Madhurāvijayam,
or
Vīrakamparāyacarita

Women's Writings in Sanskrit Literature, vol. 4

Madhurāvijayam, or Vīrakamparāyacarita

of Gaṅgādevī

Translated into English with Notes
by
Sujatha Reddy

DK PRINTWORLD
Publishers of Indian Traditions

Cataloging in Publication Data — DK
[Courtesy: D.K. Agencies (P) Ltd. <docinfo@dkagencies.com>]

Gaṅgādevi, active 14th century, **author**.
[Madhurāvijaya. English]
Madhurāvijayam, or, Vīrakamparāyacarita of Gaṅgādevī / translated with notes by Sujatha Reddy.
pages cm – (Women's writings in Sanskrit literature ; vol. 4)
Poems.
Translated from Sanskrit.
Includes bibliographical references.
ISBN 9788124610626

1. Kaṁparāya, active 14th century – Poetry. 2. Epic poetry, Sanskrit – Translations into English. I. Reddy, Sujatha, translator, editor. II. Title. III. Title: Vīrakaṁparāyacarita of Gaṅgādevī. IV. Series: Women's writings in Sanskrit literature ; vol. 4.

LCC PK3794.G33M3 2021 | DDC 891.21 23

ISBN: 978-81-246-1062-6
First published in India, 2021

The publication of this book has been financially supported by the Indian Council of Historical Research. The responsibility for the facts stated or opinions expressed is entirely of the author and not of the ICHR.

Printed and published by:
D.K. Printworld (P) Ltd.
Regd. Office: "Vedaśrī", F-395, Sudarshan Park
(Metro Station: ESI Hospital) New Delhi - 110015
Phones: (011) 2545 3975, 2546 6019
e-mail: indology@dkprintworld.com
Web: www.dkprintworld.com

Acknowledgements

Madhurāvijayam of Gaṅgādevī is the fourth volume in the series of Women Writings in Sanskrit Literature.

Most of the critiques treat *Madhurāvijayam* as a historical text which has become conventional in time and space. However, this is the most popular text in women writings in Sanskrit literature. Almost every Sanskrit scholar quoted this text when the historicity of Sanskrit texts and the question of women authors are discussed. This medieval text is well known among the Sanskrit scholars.

Thanks are due to friends and scholars who helped me translate *Madhurāvijayam*. As usual, there were difficulties in locating surviving copies of earlier editions of the text. I am thankful to the earlier editors for their introduction and notes.

Translation of this poem of Gaṅgādevī of early fourteenth century, south India, was a project for my post-doctoral studies at National Institute of Advanced Studies, Bengaluru, in association with Indian Council of Historical Research (ICHR), New Delhi. My sincere thanks to ICHR for financially assisting me to do the fieldwork and to carry out the project. I am grateful to my colleagues at Indira Gandhi National Centre for the Arts (IGNCA): Dr Kalyana Chakravarthy helped me to work at Southern Regional Centre, which gave me a larger vision of the text and Professor S. Settar and Professor G.C. Tripathi's liberal discussions on the text gave me a wider analytical vision. Thanks to Susheel K. Mittal of D.K. Printworld for publishing this volume.

I dedicate this work of women writers in Sanskrit to my maternal grandmother Bidaraguppe Akkamma Munireddy, for her lingering memories.

21 March 2021 **Sujatha Reddy**

Contents

Introduction

Manuscripts

MANUSCRIPTS of *Madhurāvijayam* (*MV*) are found at Trivandrum along with the collection of *Siddhārthacarita* or *Padyacūḍāmaṇi* and a portion of another drama of unknown name. This manuscript starts from the 109th leaf and ends at 169th leaf. This primarily forms only five cantos but there are other fragmentary portions by which it makes to nine cantos and is evident that much of the portions of this manuscript have been lost. This manuscript belonged to a *paṇḍit* named Rāmaswāmī Sāstrī, the curator of publication of Sanskrit works of Trivandrum. This was discovered in the year 1914 and later was edited by G. Harihara Sāstrī, and V. Śrīnivāsa Sāstrī, dated 10 October 1916. Since then there are several editions of *Madhurāvijayam* in Sanskrit as well as other south Indian languages such as Kannada, Telugu and Tamil and this was first translated to English by Tiruvenkatachari on 6 November 1956 from Karaikudi, in Kerala. In 1969 this poem was published by Potukuchi Subrahmanya Sastri with an elaborate and scholarly commentary in Sanskrit. Subrahmanya Sastri also attempted to fill the gaps metrically of the incomplete stanzas.

About the Author: Gaṅgādevi

A typical interest of this biographical poem (*carita-kāvya*) is that its author, Gaṅgādevī is known to be the wife of King Kampana whom it eulogizes and that in all probability she accompanied her husband in his sojourns to the south. She was the chief queen of Kampana, and though nothing is known about her lineage, she was from a royal family as the suffix *devī* would imply and she was a Āndhra princess belonging to Kākatīya lineage. She is described as being very highly accomplished and endowed with all charms and grace as such. Kampana has lavished all his love and attention on her though he had other wives. The text records her name in the seventh canto of the work:

> Then the devoted king Kampana duly performed the worship of *sandhyā* and afterwards addressed his queen who was near and whom the world was overjoyed to call her as Gaṅgā. – *MV* 7.39

Generally, there is not much known about the Sanskrit poets. In fact, they talk very less or nothing about their personal life in *kāvya*s. In Sanskrit religion and philosophy, it is considered as their work is due to the grace of God and it is not appropriate to praise themselves above the divine power or God's supremacy. But Gaṅgādevī is an exception to this general rule. Unlike several other Sanskrit authors, she has indeed given us considerable information about her ancestors, her original home, education and the date of her work *Madhurāvijayam*.

As we have seen earlier, Gaṅgādevī was an Āndhra princess belonging to Kākatīya lineage born in a place near Orugallu, present-day Warangal and she was a Telugu-speaking lady, in all probability, she knew Kannada also since the court language of the Saṅgama dynasty was Kannada. In or about 1340 CE, she had the privilege of being the queen of Vīra-Kampana, king of Karnataka–Āndhra. As has been said before, Gaṅgādevī has been accepted as a contemporary of Viśvanātha who lived during the period 1294–1325 CE. He was the court poet of King Pratāpa Rudradeva who lived during 1296–1325 CE. On the basis of this, we can say that Gaṅgādevī must have lived in a period, 1301–1400 CE. Gaṅgādevī mentions the name of Gaṅgādahara who flourished during 1250–1350 CE. She mentions the name, of Agastya who lived during the period 1275–1325 CE. She also mentions the name of Tikkayya who lived during 1290–1350 CE. It shows that Gaṅgādevī lived in the same period and she was influenced by all them as she praises them in the first canto of this work.

Structure of the Text

Structure of the text is very simple, written in Dvipada style, meaning verse of two lines. Each chapter is written in a particular metre along with various *śabda* and *arthālaṁkāra*s, such as Rūpaka, Upamā and Dṛṣṭānta. The metres used in the nine cantos of the text are Anuṣṭubh, Upajāti, Vaṁśastha, Drutavilambita, Puṣpitāgra, Viyoginī; Aupachandasika and Indravarjā, respectively from cantos one to nine.

Gaṅgādevī also introduces many poets and their contributions. She inculcates characters of these poets' works in her work: she follows Viśvanātha in characterizing poetic embellishments such as *rasa* and also follows Kālidāsa. Thus, it stands as a good example of the *mahākāvya* genre in Sanskrit. It engages the attention of the readers with its noble theme of description of various items and delineation of the different *rasa*s with Vīra as the predominant *rasa*. The poetical genius of these and the moral fervour and zeal usually associated with religious teachers, produced a host of literary works of great merit, thus making an abiding contribution to the literary heritage, secular as well as sectarian, of the early Vijayanagara period.

However, The text after fifth canto is not consistent; there are a number of breaks and textual verses are missing from various places and also at times incomplete. Hence the text loses its original sheen in narrations and descriptions at many places. Here, it should be noted that the text should have been larger than the now available edition.

Date of the Text

Madhurāvijayam can be conveniently dated to 1373-75 CE because as per the text, the conquest of Madurai took place about 1365-71 CE, and also it is evident from the description of the war in the text that Gaṅgādevī herself might have accompanied King Kampana to the war field. (For more discussion, refer to Textual Analysis.)

श्रीगङ्गादेव्या विरचितम्

मधुराविजयम्

अथवा

वीरकम्परायचरितं

प्रथमः सर्गः

Canto 1

कल्याणाय सतां भूयात् देवो दन्तावलाननः ।
शरणागतसङ्कल्प कल्पनाकल्पपादपः ।।१।।

Let it be prosperous to God, who has protruded teeth in the face (Gaṇeśa), whose form is like the kalpa plants, fulfils the desires of the shelter seekers of those who surrender to his elegance, be auspicious to the good. (1)

स्रष्टुः स्त्री [पुंसनिर्मा*]णमातृकारूपधारिणौ ।
प्रपद्ये प्रतिबोधाय चित्प्रकाशात्मकौ शिवौ ।।२।।

Meant for attaining knowledge in the creation who has adored in the forms of man and woman that God Śiva and his wife, who personify the universal consciousness I pray to them and entirely come near to them. (2)

महाकविमुखाम्भोज मणिपञ्जरशारिकाम् ।
चैतन्यजलधिज्योत्स्नां देवीं वन्दे सरस्वतीम् ।।३।।

I bow to Goddess Sarasvatī who lives in the lotus-like mouths of great poets as a *sārikā* bird, in a jewelled cage, and who operates like moonlight on the ocean of intellect. (3)

असाधारणसार्वज्ञ्यं विलसत्सर्वमङ्गलम् ।
क्रियाशक्तिगुरुं वन्दे त्रिलोचनमिवापरम् ।।४।।

I bow to teacher Kriyāśakti who has the great knowledge and to Goddess Sarvamaṅgalā who spends time with Trilocana who shines besides her. (4)

चेतसोऽस्तु प्रसादाय सतां **प्राचेतसो** मुनिः ।
पृथिव्यां पद्यनिर्माणविद्यायाः प्रथमे पदम् ।।५।।

May Sage Prācetasa who first set the erudition of creating poetry on earth, let him bring cheerfulness to the minds of the virtuous. (5)

वैयासिके गिरां गुम्फे पुण्ड्रेक्षाविव लभ्यते ।
सद्यः सहृदयाह्लादी सारः पर्वणि पर्वणि ।।६।।

In every section of Vyāsa's sequence of expressions (the *Mahābhārata*), like the delicious juice in every joint of red sugar cane, There is sweet essence which convey immediate enjoyment to men of good taste. (6)

दासतां **कालिदासस्य** कवयः के न बिभ्रति।
इदानीमपि तस्यार्थानुपजीवन्त्यमी यतः ।।७।।

Who are the poets who do not play the role of a slave to Kālidāsa? For, even the current poets live by his ideas. (7)

वाणीपाणिपरामृष्टवीणानिक्वाणहारिणीम् ।
भावयन्ति कथं वान्ये **भट्टबाणस्य भारतीम्** ।।८।।

How could others grasp the expressiveness of Bāṇa Bhaṭṭa which captivates like the musical sound of the lute played by Sarasvatī's own hand. (8)

विमर्दव्यक्तसौरभ्या भारती **भारवेः** कवेः ।
धत्ते वकुलमालेव विदग्धानां चमत्क्रियाम् ।।९।।

Just as the garland of *vakulā* flowers yields its sweet scent only when pressed, so too, the language of Bhāravi reveals its brilliance and gives delight to the erudite only if they perceive it. (9)

आचार्यदण्डिनो वाचामाचान्तामृतसंपदाम् ।
विकासो वेधसः पत्न्या विलासमणिदर्पणः ।।१०।।

Thriving of expressions of Ācārya Daṇḍin drunk (as it were) with the wealth of nectar, sparkle like the elegant precious gem-studded mirror of the creator's consort. (10)

सा कापि सुरभिः शङ्के **भवभूतेः** सरस्वती ।
कर्णेषु लब्धवर्णानां सूते सुखमयीं सुधाम् ।।११।।

I believe that Bhavabhūti's masterpieces must be some variety of Kāmadhenu, for they produce in the ears of the scholars a pleasure akin to the consumption of nectar. (11)

मन्दारमञ्जरीस्यन्दिमकरन्दरसाब्धयः ।
कस्य नाह्लादनायालं **कर्णामृतकवेर्गिरः** ।।१२।।

Whom would the expressions of the poet of *Karṇāmṛta* fail to enchant by the expression of words like the ocean of honey flowing from the flower clusters of the *mandāra* tree? (12)

तिक्कयस्य कवेः सूक्तिः कौमुदीव कलानिधेः ।
सतृष्णैः कविभिः स्वैरं चकोरैरिव सेव्यते ।।१३।।

Even as the thirsty *cakora* birds love to drink the rays of the moon, poets find immense relishment in the poetic sayings of Tikkayya. (13)

चतुस्सप्ततिकाव्योक्तिव्यक्तवैदुष्यसंपदे ।
अगस्त्याय जगत्यस्मिन् स्पृहयेत् को न कोविदः ।।१४।।

Who will not be jealous of the breathless (writings) of the man of learning of the poet Agastya whose wealth of learning is established by the creation of as many as seventy-four poetic compositions? (14)

स्तुमस्तमपरं व्यासं **गङ्गाधर**महाकविम् ।
नाटकच्छद्मना दृष्टां यश्चक्रे भारतीं कथाम् ।।१५।।

We reverentially treat the great poet Gaṅgādhara as the second Vyāsa. In that he has made the story of the Bharata as the visual poetry – which enacted as drama. (15)

चिरं स विजयीभूयाद् **विश्वनाथः** कवीश्वरः ।
यस्य प्रसादात् सार्वज्ञ्यं समिन्धे मादृशेष्वपि ।।१६।।

May the lord of the poet Viśvanātha prosper for long, it is by his grace, even in individuals like myself, has dawned an everlasting sense of poetry. (16)

क्वचिदर्थः क्वचिच्छब्दः क्वचिद् भावः क्वचिद् रसः ।
यत्रैते सन्ति सर्वेऽपि स निबन्धो न लभ्यते ।।१७।।

There is wisdom in some, idea in some and emotion in some, but nowhere to found a work where all these be present together. (17)

प्रबन्धमीषन्मात्रोऽपि दोषो नयति दूष्यताम् ।
कालागरुद्रवभरं शुक्तिक्षारकणो यथा ।।१८।।

Even as a single sour particle from an oyster shell spoils the liquid essence of the black *agāru*, so too even the negligible blemish found in a *prabandha* makes it reproachable. (18)

निर्दोषाप्यगुणा वाणी न विद्वज्जनरञ्जिनी ।
पतिव्रताप्यरूपा स्त्री परिणेत्रे न रोचते ।।१९।।

Just as an unattractive woman, though virtuous, is not pleasing to her husband, a flawless poetic composition, if devoid of characters (poetry), does not satisfy the erudite men. (19)

गुणं विहाय काव्येषु दुष्टो दोषं गवेषते ।
वनेषु त्यक्तमाकन्दः काको निम्बमपेक्षते ।।२०।।

A despicable man searches for faults in a poetic composition in disregard of its merits. Like the crow shows a preference to the *nimba* fruit and dislikes a mango fruit in the forest. (20)

चौर्यार्जितेन काव्येन कियद् दीव्यति दुर्जनः ।
आहार्यरागो न चिरं रुचिरः कृत्रिमोपलः ।।२१।।

How long can a plagiarist obtain poetry by stealing? For, short-lived is the radiance of false colouring in an artificial stone. (21)

तार्किका बहवः सन्ति शाब्दिकाश्च सहस्रशः ।
विरलाः कवयो लोके सरलालापपेशलाः ।।२२।।

Logicians are many; grammarians flourish in thousands, but scarcely can be found poets who are appealing by the source of their beautiful simple opinions. (22)

करोति कीर्तिमर्थाय कल्पते हन्ति दुष्कृतम् ।
उन्मीलयति चाह्लादं किं न सूते कवेः कृतिः ।।२३।।

Good poetry promotes fame; serves for wealth, destroys immorality and awakens delight. What is that the good poetry does not capitulate? (23)

न प्रार्थनीयः सत्काव्यश्रुत्यै सहृदयो जनः ।
स्वादुपुष्परसास्वादे कः प्रेरयति षट्पदम् ।।२४।।

Not prayed to listen to the good poetry by the gentle learned people. Who urges the bee to taste the honey in the flower? (24)

तन्मदीयमिदं काव्यं विबुधाः! श्रोतुमर्हथ ।
मधुराविजयं नाम चरितं **कम्पभूपतेः** ।।२५।।

Learned men, please listen therefore to this poem of mine dealing with the life of king Kampana, going by the famous title of the conquest of Madhurā. (25)

आसीत् समस्तसामन्तमस्तकन्यस्तशासनः ।
बुक्कराज इति ख्यातो राजा **हरिहरानुजः** ।।२६।।

There was a famous king called Bukka who was the younger brother of Harihara and whose orders were abide the vassals they bear these orders on their heads; they were all the neighbouring vassals. (26)

यः शेष इव नागानां नगानां हिमवानिव ।
दैत्यारिरिव देवानां प्रथमः पृथिवीभुजाम् ।।२७।।

Like Śeṣa among serpents, Himavān among mountains and enemy of demons (Viṣṇu) among gods, he occupied the first place among the lords of the earth. (27)

तिग्मांशोरपि तेजस्वी शीतांशोरपि शीतलः ।
सागरादपि गम्भीरः सुमेरोरपि यः स्थिरः ।।२८।।

Severe than the sun and he is pleasing than the moon. In

profundity he surpass the ocean, and he is firm like the mount Sumeru. (28)

विवेकमेव सचिवं धनुरेव वरूथिनीम् ।
बाहुमेव रणोत्साहे यः सहायममन्यत ।।२९।।

He has wise ministers, he has the strong bow and (fights) alone for his army, he counted on his arms as his only assistant in the battle is his enthusiastic heart. (He does not seek help from others.) (29)

जिष्णुना भुवनेशेन श्रीदेन समवर्तिना ।
सान्निध्यं लोकपालानां धरणौ येन दर्शितम् ।।३०।।

He established the existence of the (four) guardian deities of the universe even on this earth, by being victorious (like Indra), by being the overlord of the waters (like Varuṇa), by giving away wealth (like Kubera) and by being impartial (like Yama). (30)

हृदये चन्दनालेपैः कर्णे मौक्तिककुण्डलैः ।
सतां मुखे च कर्पूरैर्यस्याभावि यशोभरैः ।।३१।।

His immense fame spread like the smell of the sandal paste smeared on his chest; he wearing pearl earrings in the ears; smearing the camphor powder on the faces. (31)

विरोधिवाहिनीनाथविक्षोभणपटीयसा ।
भुजेन भूभृता यस्य प्राप्ता कीर्तिमयी सुधा ।।३२।।

By the might of his arm which perplexed the army generals of his enemies; fame was won by him, like the nectar of fame was churned by his shoulders. (32)

यस्य कीर्त्या प्रसर्पन्त्या गुणकर्पूरशालिनः ।
जगदण्डकरण्डस्य क्षौमकञ्चुलिकायितम् ।।३३।।

His fame as a person of charming qualities was all-encompassing; that it appeared like cover of white silk on the egg-shaped universe. (33)

परिपन्थिनृपप्राणपवनाहारदारुणः ।
असृजद् भुजगो यस्य कृपाणः कीर्तिकञ्चुकम् ।।३४।।

The sword exerted by his hand looked terrible as if it is feasting on the life breath of his royal enemies, he attained glory, even as a ferocious serpent, feeding on air, produces its cover and slough it off. (34)

यदीयो दक्षिणः पाणिः कृपाणीग्रहणच्छलात् ।
अशिक्षत विपक्षश्रीवेणीकर्षणकौशलम् ।।३५।।

His right hand which to all appearance seemed to be drawing the sword was in fact enthusiastic in the art of dragging the braided hair of the goddesses of prosperity of his adversaries. (35)

लक्ष्मीश्चिराज्जगद्रक्षाजागरूकमुपेत्य यम् ।
योगनिद्राजडं विष्णुं कदाचिदपि नास्मरत् ।।३६।।

Goddess Lakṣmī having after a long time come to him who is always awake in defending the earth, never again remembered Viṣṇu who was insensitive and enveloped in yogic sleep. (36)

कलिकालमहाघर्मप्लुष्टो धर्ममहीरुहः ।
यस्य दानाम्बुसेकेन पुनरङ्कुरितोऽभवत् ।।३७।।

The tree of *dharma,* which had shrunken by the blazing heat of the Kali Age, sprouted again by the water that flowed (from his hands) while giving the donations. (37)

यस्याङ्घ्रिपीठसंघर्षरेखालाञ्छितमौलयः ।
आशास्वरिनृपा एव जयस्तम्भतया स्थिताः ।।३८।।

His enemy kings, who bore on their head scars developed by rubbing against his foot rest, were looked like the many pillars of triumph in all directions. (38)

यत्प्रतापानलज्वालामालाकबलिता इव ।
कीर्तयः शत्रुभूपानामासन् मलिनमूर्तयः ।।३९।।

The status of his adversaries as if they were enclosed by rows of flames of the fire of his prowess looked dark in appearance. (39)

बद्धाः सभाङ्गणे यस्य भान्ति स्म जयसिन्धुराः ।
बन्दीकृता इवाम्भोदा जैत्रयात्रानिरोधिनः ।।४०।।

As if chained in the entrance of the court hall his victorious elephants looked like confined dark clouds, and were looking like opposing the expeditions again. (40)

यस्य सेनातुरङ्गाणां खुरैरुत्थापितं रजः ।
अकाण्डे राहुसन्देहं मार्ताण्डस्योदपादयत् ।।४१।।

Dust raised by the hoofs of warhorses like clouds made the sun apprehensive of an unexpectedly sudden approach of Rāhu. (41)

यद्विभूतिस्तुतौ स्वल्पा लक्ष्मीर्यक्षामरेशयोः ।
दूरे दुर्योधनादीनां संपत्सादृश्यकल्पना ।।४२।।

As against his prosperity, the prosperity of Indra looked trivial and far remote became the question of any comparison between the fortune of personality like Duryodhana and him. (42)

(The city of Vijayanagara.)

तस्यासीद् विजया नाम विजयार्जितसंपदः ।
राजधानी बुधैः श्लाघ्या शक्रस्थेवामरावती ।।४३।।

He who augmented his riches by victory had the famous Vijaya named capital city. That city won the approval of knowing men and praised as Śakra's Amarāvatī. (43)

सुरलोकान्तसंक्रान्तस्वर्णदीमत्सरादिव ।
परिस्वाकारतां यान्त्या परीता तुङ्गभद्रया ।।४४।।

As if in rivalry with the heavenly waters that flowed round the borders of heaven, River Tuṅgabhadrā surrounded the city as a terrible moat. (44)

लक्ष्मीलतालवालेन क्ष्मावधूनाभिशोभिना ।
चक्राचलप्रकारेण प्राकारेण परिष्कृता ।।४५।।

The city was also surrounded by ramparts on all sides which were high as the Cakrācala mountains and it had the beauty of the water channels surrounded by the Lakṣmī creeper and looked like the navel of Goddess Earth. (45)

स्फुरन्मणिप्रमाहूतपुरुहूतशरासनैः ।
सुमेरुशृङ्गसंकाशैर्गोपुरैरुपशोभिता ।।४६।।

Lofty and gem-set towers, like the peaks of the mount Sumeru emanating rainbow colours, ornamented the city. (46)

उत्फुल्लचम्पकाशोकनागकेसरकेसरैः ।
वसन्तबासभवनैरारागैरभितो वृता ।।४७।।

The city was also surrounded by pleasure gardens which looked like the dwelling place of spring and which were full of flowering trees like *campaka*, *aśoka*, *nāga* and *kesara,* discharging fresh pollens. (47)

कस्तूरीहरिणाक्रान्तकर्पूरकदलीतलैः ।
मनोभवमहीदुर्गैर्महिता केलिपर्वतैः ।।४८।।

The pleasure mountains in the city were frequented by the musk deer that sought the shade of the banana plants and *karpūra* plants in these hillocks looked like the genuine hiding place of the god of love. (48)

कमलामोदमधुरैः कलहंसकुलाकुलैः ।
क्रीडासरोभिः सहिता मणिसोपानमञ्जुलैः ।।४९।।

The city had sporting lakes filled with fragrant waters of lotuses. These lakes had gem-studded steps and were always occupied by beautiful swans. (49)

यशस्स्तोमैरिवाशेषनगरीविजयार्जितैः ।
सौधैः प्रकाशितोत्सेधा शरदम्भोदपाण्डरैः ।।५०।।

The elevated portions of the city had high-built palaces which were white like the autumn clouds. One surprised they were so many shapes like the fame of the king who conquered all cities. (50)

विकसद्वनितावल्लीविलासवनवाटिका ।
दक्षिणाशासरोजाक्षीफाललीलाललाटिका ।।५१।।

The city looked like the stage set for flowering trees and displaying the pleasant beauty of the women or it may even be depicted as the mark of fashion and exquisiteness embellishing the forehead of the lady known as earth's southern part. (51)

द्विजराजसमुल्लासनित्यराकानिशीथिनी।
गन्धर्वगणसान्निध्यनव्यदिव्यवरूथिनी ।।५२।।

The city was full of virtuous brāhmaṇas and mass of musicians who freely walk in its open grounds. It's like the full-moon night along with the world of celestial bards, with full of serenity and continuous music swayed all over. (52)

भुजङ्गसङ्गसंवासभूतेशमुकुटस्थली ।
सुमनस्स्तोमसंचारसुवर्णगिरिमेखला ।।५३।।

*Bhujaṅga*s (the fashionable youth) made that city their beloved haunt, like the *bhunjaṅga*s (serpents) made the crown of Śiva their chosen dwelling. Virtuous people in large numbers loved to stroll in its grounds like the gods in the regions of Sumeru. (53)

लीलेव दिष्टिवृद्धीनां शालेव सकलश्रियाम् ।
मालेव सर्वरत्नानां वेलेय सुकृताम्बुधेः ।।५४।।
(द्वादशभिः कुलकम् ।)

The city was the playground of all good wealth and opulence in all its aspects, people were delighted to live in its public houses. The city looked like a garland of precious stones on the shores of the sea of virtue. (54)

यस्यां प्रासादशृङ्गेषु लग्नं मार्तण्डमण्डलम् ।
संधत्ते वीक्षमाणानां सौवर्णकलशभ्रमम् ।।५५।।

The disc of the sun caught in between the lofty city's mansions for the onlookers produced the vision of golden pitcher. (55)

यत्सौधचन्द्रशालासु विहरन्त्यो मृगेक्षणाः ।
शशाङ्कमवलम्बन्ते मुक्ताकन्दुकशङ्कया ।।५६।।

The young women playing on the terrace of the top floor of the city's mansions often laid their hands on the curved body of the moon, mistaking it for their play-ball of pearls. (56)

यत्र सौधेषु सङ्गीतमृदङ्गप्रतिनादिषु ।
अकाण्डे ताण्डवारम्भं वितन्वन्ति शिखण्डिनः ।।५७।।

Hearing the sound of the beats of drum accompanying the music played in the city's mansions, the peacock began to dance even in the absence of any proper occasion. (Such as the appearance of thunder in the clouds.) (57)

पद्मरागोपलोत्कीर्णप्रासादप्रान्तवर्तिनः ।
सन्ततं यत्र दृश्यन्ते सान्ध्या इव बलाहकाः ।।५८।।

The clouds that hung on the sides of the city's mansions, reflecting the colour of the *padmarāga* gems, reflected in them, always looked dark hued like evening clouds. (58)

सन्ध्यासु यत्र निर्यान्ति जालेभ्यो धूपराजयः ।
अन्तःप्रदीपिकालोकचकितध्वान्तसन्निभाः ।।५९।।

The clouds of smoke that emanated through the cervices in the buildings of the city at the evening time appeared like darkness affecting its escape afraid of being caught in the shine while impending lamplight inside. (59)

यद्दीर्घिकासु माणिक्क्मयसोपानचारिभिः ।
क्षणदास्वपि चक्राह्वैर्विरहो नानुभूयते ।।६०।।

As the lustre of the gems with which the steps were paved in the lakes always drove darkness away leaving the *cakravāka* birds there who were not separated even at nightfall. (60)

यदङ्गनामुखाम्भोजलावण्यालाभलज्जितः ।
कलङ्कच्छद्मना चन्द्रो व्यनक्ति हृदयव्यथाम् ।।६१।।

The moon, as if embarrassed by the shimmering beauty marking the lotus-like faces of the lovely women in the city, ever carried a mourning black on her body known as *kalaṅka*. (61)

यत्र स्त्रीणां कटाक्षेषु यूनां हृदयहारिषु ।
पुष्पास्त्रसंचये वाञ्छां मुञ्चते पञ्चसायकः ।।६२।।

The god of love never contemplated of resorting to his flower arrows to effect his victories in the face of the lovely glances shot from the eyes of beautiful women there to restrain the hearts of youth. (62)

मरालैर्मञ्जुमञ्जीरशिञ्जिताकृष्टमानसैः ।
लीलागतिमिव प्राप्तुं सेव्यन्ते यत्र योषितः ।।६३।।

As if to take their lessons in elegant walking the swans ever wanted the company of women there, engrossed by the sweet jingling noise of their foot-ornaments. (63)

यत्रावलग्नसादृश्यवाञ्छाविमतमम्बरम् ।
प्रायः पयोधरोत्सेधैर्निरुन्धन्ति पुरन्ध्रयः ।।६४।।

The blossoming breasts of the maidens of the city were wonderfully set off their slender waists in between the thick black hair like the thick clouds in the upper sky. (64)

यत्र वामभ्रुवामेव काठिन्यं स्तनमण्डले ।
कौटिल्यं कबरीमारे कार्श्यं मध्ये च दृश्यते ।।६५।।

As there was no rigidity there in the city except in the breasts of beautiful damsels, nor crookedness except in their curly locks, nor thinness except in their waists. (65)

यच्छाखानगरीं **पम्पा**मनेकधनदाश्रिताम् ।
अधितिष्ठन् **विरूपाक्षो** न स्मरत्यलंकापुरीम् ।।६६।।

Pampā was the branch city of Vijaya. Many wealthy lords lived there so much so that God Virūpākṣa who was enshrined there never thought about his original home at the city of Alakā. (66)

स तस्याममरावत्यां पुरुहूत इव स्थितः ।
अशिषद् द्यामिव क्षोणीमनवद्यपराक्रमः ।।६७।।

Installed in that city, he of his undiminished ability, ruled over the earth even as Indra (Puruhūta) ruled the heavenly regions from his seat in Amarāvatī. (67)

मित्राभ्युदयदायिन्या भूत्या नीत्या प्रभूतया ।
मनुमेव पुनर्जातं तममन्यन्त मानवाः ।।६८।।

By considering his prosperity that was at the service of his friends and his politics, that was wide and complete, his subjects imagined that Manu himself has taken his second birth. (68)

समोऽपि पुरुषार्थेषु स धर्मं सम्मतः सताम् ।
बह्वमंस्त पुमानाद्यः सत्वं त्रिषु गुणेष्विव ।।६९।।

Though unbiased to all the three *puruṣārtha*s – *dharma*, *artha* and *kāma* – the king who was the idol of all righteous people had a special regard for *dharma* (like Viṣṇu), the lord of all, who has for *sattva* (*guṇa* as prominent), among his three *guṇa*s – *sattva*, *rajas* and *tamas*. (69)

दानं पाणेः श्रुतेः सूक्तं मौलेस्त्र्यम्बकपादुकाम् ।
भूषाममंस्त यः [श्रीमान् श्रेयोऽवाप्तिसमुत्सुकः*] ।।७०।।

His hands were meant for donations, his ears heard the sayings of the Śāstras well, his head was always crowned with the *pāduka*s (footwear) of Lord Śiva. The wisdom of ornamental superiority that he thereby evinced became the means of his attainment and desire to get and keep his prosperity. (70)

आ विन्ध्यादा च मलयादास्ताद्रेरा च रोहणात् ।
प्रकम्पिताहितप्राणं प्राणंसिषुरमुं नृपाः ॥७१॥

The kings that ruled over the regions of which the mountains of Vindhya, Malayā, Astā and Rohaṇa were the four boundaries whose kings paid homage to him, and those that were enemies were shaken with fear. (71)

कुलक्रमानु[संप्राप्तक्षोणीरक्षणजा*] गरः ।
अभुङ्क्त विपुलान् भोगाननासक्तमनाः प्रभुः ॥७२॥

Always aware of his duty of guarding the kingdom that came to him from his ancestors in an unbroken line of succession, the king enjoyed the immense pleasure befitting his royal rank hitherto with complete objectivity. (72)

देवायी नाम तस्यासीद् देवी वसुमतीपतेः ।
पद्मा पद्मेक्षणस्येव शङ्करस्येव पार्वती ॥७३॥

Like Lakṣmī to Nārāyaṇa (lotus eyed) and Pārvatī to Śaṅkara, Queen Devāyī was to the king (Vasumatī-Pati) and she is the chosen consort. (73)

सत्स्वप्यन्येषु दारेषु तामेव मनुजाधिपः ।
वह्वमंस्त निशानाथो नक्षत्रेष्विव रोहिणीम् ॥७४॥

Though the king had other wives also, she alone became the object of his love and regard, even as Rohiṇī to the moon among celestial personalities. (74)

कर्णाटलोकनयनोत्सवपूर्णचन्द्रः
साकं तया हृदयसंमतया नरेन्द्रः ।
कालोचितान्यनुभवन् क्रमशः सुखानि
वीरश्चिराय **विजयापुर**मध्यवात्सीत् ॥७५॥

The brave king who was pleasing like the full moon to the eyes of the people of Karṇāta dwelt along at the city of Vijayāpura and enjoyed the delights of his youth with her who was his heart's beloved. (75)

।। इति श्रीगङ्गादेव्या विरचिते मधुराविजयम्-
नाम्नि वीरकम्परायचरिते प्रथमः सर्गः।।

Thus ends the first canto, of the life of Vīra Kamparāya known as *Madhurāvijayam* composed by Śrī Gaṅgā Devī.

मीनाक्ष्यै नमः

Salutation to Goddess Mināksị̄

द्वितीयः सर्गः

Canto 2

अथास्य वंशप्रतिरोहबीजं महीभुजो गर्भमधत्त देवी ।
जगत्त्रयोद्भूतिनिदानभूतं तेजो विधातुः प्रथमेव सृष्टिः ।।१।।

The queen conceived by the king and bore in her womb, the seed of royal race, as the celestial waters held in them the brilliance and virility of Vidhātā (Brahmā) with which the three worlds were created. (1)

मुखेन तन्वी शरपाण्डरेण विमुक्तरत्नाभरणा विरेजे ।
विलूनराजीववना दिनान्ते छायाशशाङ्केन शरन्नदीव ।।२।।

The queen put aside her jewels; her face was somewhat pale like the *śara* reed and her form unusually slender. She shined like a river in autumn where lotuses disappeared and with the sphere of the moon reflected on its watery surface. (2)

गर्भस्थितस्येव शिशोर्विधातुं वसुन्धरामण्डलमारशिक्षाम् ।
अरोचयत् पार्थिवधर्मपत्नी मन्ये मृदास्वादरसानुबन्धम् ।।३।।

She who was the adored wife of the lord of this earth indulged in experience units of it as if to teach the responsibility of earth to the infant through the sways in her womb. (3)

अनन्यसामान्यभुजापदानमुत्पत्स्यमानं तनयं नृपस्य ।
अनारतं वीररसानुबन्धं न्यवेदयद् दौहृदमेव देव्याः ।।४।।

The very character of her yearnings in her pregnancy which always took courageous turn suggested that her would-be son would be committed to heroic events. (4)

सा **तुङ्गभद्रां** सविधे वहन्तीं सुभ्रूरनादृत्य सुखावगाहाम् ।
विहर्तुमैच्छन्निजसैन्यनागैस्तरङ्गिते वारिणि **ताम्रपर्ण्याः** ।।५।।

Without considering River Tuṅgabhadrā which flowed nearby and which was easily fordable she desired to sport in the

Tāmraparṇī in the company of her army of elephants that would raise waves in its waters. (While they played in the water.) (5)

अपारयन्ती चरितैणशाबं क्रीडाचलोपान्तमपि प्रयातुम् ।
आखेटरागादधिरोढुमैच्छन्माद्यन्मृगेन्द्रान् **मलयाद्रिकूटान्** ।।६।।

Though she was physically unable to walk as far as the pleasure hill where the deer were quietly grazing, she in her mental flights was on the pinnacle of the Malaya Mountain populated by ferocious lions. (6)

सा दैत्यनाथप्रथनाय पूर्वं विष्णोरधस्तात्कृतपौरुषस्य ।
आकर्णयन्ती कुहनाप्रपञ्चादासी.................।।७।।

She heard of Viṣṇu's marvellous exploits of crushing the demon kings on the earth and wanted to imitate him. (7)

पृथ्वी रथः सारथिरब्जसूतिः शेषेण सज्यं धनुरद्रिराजः ।
शरश्च शौरिः किल हन्त लक्ष्यं त्रयं पुरामित्यहसत् पुरारिम् ।।८।।

She laughed at Śiva's courage in reducing Tripurā aided by all such belongings as the earth as the chariot, Brahmā as the charioteer, Śeṣa as bowstring, the mountain as the bow and Hari as the arrow. (8)

क्रमाज्जहद्भिः क्रशिमानमङ्गैर्मुखेन मुग्धालसलोचनेन ।
मध्येन च (व्य?त्य)क्तवलित्रयेण नरेश्वरं नन्दयति स्म राज्ञी ।।९।।

As time advanced the limbs of her body began to put on flesh, her face resumed its sweet and lazy eye looks, her belly began to show its crease distinctly and this change in his beloved filled the king with enchantment. (9)

सौभाग्यगन्धद्विपदानलेखा रराज तस्या नवरोमराजिः ।
तेजोनिधिं गर्भतले निगूढं कालोरगी रक्षितुमागतेव ।।१०।।

The propitious line of hair that was on her abdomen looked like black serpent on watch in order to protect the infant within. (10)

श्यामायमानच्छविना मुखेन स्तनद्वयं तामरसेक्षणायाः ।
संदष्टनीलोत्पलयोरमित्यां रथाङ्गनाम्नोरधरीचकार ।।११।।

Her breasts with black nipples surpassed in their prettiness the *cakravāka* couple with a bit of blue *utpala* (*Nymphea alba* – white water rose resembleing lilly) flower in the beaks. (11)

तामम्बुगर्भामिव मेघमालां वेलामिवाभ्यन्तरलीनचन्द्राम ।
अन्तस्स्थरत्नामिव शुक्तिरेखामापन्नसत्त्वां प्रभुरभ्यनन्दत् ।।१२।।

The lord of earth regarded her being in an exciting state, like as if she were a rain cloud full of water or a pearl oyster with pearl inside and night time through whole revelation slowed down the rise of the moon. (12)

ततः परं तापहरः प्रजानां पुरोहितोक्त्या पुरुहूतकल्पः ।
व्यधत्त काले विभवानुरूपं पुंसां वरः पुंसवनक्रियां सः ।।१३।।

The king who was as prosperous as Puruhūta (Indra) and who was ever bent on the enhancement of his subjects celebrated the ceremony of *puṁsavana* (baby shower) as ordered by his priest at the appointed time on a scale befitted to his royal rank. (13)

अथ प्रशस्ते दिवसे समस्तैर्मौहूर्तिकैः साधितपुण्यलग्ने ।
अभूत सूनुं नरनाथपत्नी देवी महासेनमिवेन्दुमौलेः ।।१४।।

Then on an auspicious day at the hour manifested as most auspicious by astrologers the queen presented her lord with a boy as Goddess Pārvatī bore to Śiva. (14)

महौजसस्तस्य निजैर्यशोभिरुद्वेलदुग्धोदधिपूरगौरैः ।
प्रक्षालितानीव तदा बभूवुर्धृतप्रसादानि दिशां मुखानि ।।१५।।

The quarters then shone with spotless gleam as if they had been newly washed by royal fame which was fit to be likened to the whiteness of milk that filled the milky ocean. (15)

ज्ञात्वा वशे तस्य भुवं भवित्रीं भयादिवास्पृष्टपरागलेशः ।
आकृष्टकल्पद्रुमपुष्पगन्धो मरुद् ववौ मन्दममन्दशैत्यः ।।१६।।

Cool breeze perfumed with the flower dusts from heavenly trees began to blow gently as if afraid of the new born infant who was soon to attain the mastery of this earth. (16)

आगामिनीमध्वरहव्यसिद्धिं निश्चित्य देशेष्वपि दक्षिणेषु ।
प्रदक्षिणीभूतशिखाकलापो ननर्त हर्षादिव हव्यवाहः ॥१७॥

The god of fire seemed to dance with joy telling the auspicious circles with his bright ends and this betokened that fruitful sacrifices would soon be performed all over the southern countries in abundance. (17)

कल्पद्रुमास्तेन हरिष्यमाणां मत्वा निजां त्यागयशःपताकाम् ।
पयोधरप्रेषितपुष्पवर्षाः प्रागेव सन्धानमिवान्वतिष्ठन् ॥१८॥

The *kalpa*[1] trees by showering down flowers through clouds looked as if courting in advance the friendship of royal child who was soon to excel them in the grandeur of charity. (18)

स्ववैरिभूतान् मृगयासु सिंहान् हन्ता प्रवीरोऽयमिति प्रहर्षात् ।
प्रभिन्नगण्डस्रुतदानधारा जगर्जुरुच्चैर्जयकुञ्जरेन्द्राः ॥१९॥

The wild elephants with ichor flowing down their cheeks trumpeted in joy as if in deliberation of the destruction that awaited their enemies, the lions at the hands of the royal baby said that he would soon grow up to be a daring hunter. (19)

अस्योपवाह्यत्वमुपेत्य लभ्यां कीर्तिं भवित्रीभिव भावयन्तः ।
क्ष्मामुल्लिखन्तश्चटुलेः खुराग्रैर्जिहेषिरे हर्षजुषस्तुरङ्गाः ॥२०॥

The horses also neighed with joy scratching the ground with their large hoofs perhaps thinking that they would soon be mounted upon by the child and a great splendour anticipated them in the task. (20)

प्रस्तावितो मङ्गलतूर्यघोषैः प्रसारितश्चारणचाटुवादैः ।
प्रहृष्यतां तत्र पुरे जनानां कोलाहलः कोऽपि समुज्जजृम्भे ॥२१॥

---

1 Popularly coconut trees. There are many kalpa trees, one among them is coconut tree.

Tumultuous rejoicings among the people of the city arose with blowing trumpets and *cāraṇa*s (hailers) hailing auspiciously. (21)

सुखायमानां सुतजन्मवार्तां सहर्षमावेदयते जनाय ।
अवाञ्छदात्मानमपि प्रदातुं कुतूहली **कुन्तल**भूमिपालः ।।२२।।

The monarch of Kuntala curiously gave away all the ornaments which he wore physically to those who got the glad report of his son's birth. (22)

विशृङ्खलास्तस्य गिरा निरीयुः कारागृहेभ्यो विमतावरोधाः ।
तुलुष्कबन्दीनिवहाय तूर्णमागामिने दातुमिवावकाशम् ।।२३।।

By this royal word of command the prisons were thrown open and prisoners were unchained and liberated as if to make room for future incumbents – the Turuṣkas. (23)

स्नातस्ततो धौतदुकूलधारी वितीर्य भूरि द्रविणं द्विजेभ्यः ।
महीपतिः पुत्रमुखं दिदृक्षुः प्राविक्षदन्तःपुरमात्तहर्षः ।।२४।।

Duly bathed and clad in white silk the king after donating enormous riches as gifts to brāhmaṇas entered the bedroom of queen with a glad heart to see the face of his son. (24)

अवैक्षत क्षामशरीरयष्टेः कुमारमुत्सङ्गगतं स देव्याः ।
शरत्कृशाया इव शैवलिन्यास्तरङ्गलग्नं कलहंसशाबम् ।।२५।।

He saw the child in the lap of his slim-featured queen like a swan youngling on the wavy bed of the autumnal river. (25)

प्रकीर्णकाश्मीरपरागगौरैस्तिरस्कृताभ्यन्तरदीपशोभैः ।
निवार्यमाणं(!) मुहुरुज्जिहानैररिष्टगेहं महसां प्ररोहैः ।।२६।।

Rays of whitish light like camphor dust played on the child's form which subdued the sheen of the lamps burning in the queens chamber. (26)

मुहुर्मुहुः पल्लवपाटलेन मुष्टीकृतेन द्वितयेन पाण्योः ।
अरातिलक्ष्मीकचसंचयानामाकर्षशिक्षामिव शीलयन्तम् ।।२७।।

With his two reddish hands closed the child looked as if already practising the art of holding within his grasp the wealth goddesses of his enemies. (27)

आलक्ष्यरेखामयशङ्खचक्रच्छत्रारविन्दध्वजमीनचिह्नौ ।
प्रवालताम्राङ्गुलिदर्शनीयौ सुजातपार्ष्णी चरणौ वहन्तम् ।।२८।।

His two gracefully-shaped feet bore auspicious marks indicative of conch, disc, umbrella, lotus, banner and fish. His tiny reddish fingers, as soft as tender flora, were also beautiful to look at. (28)

का(ले?ये) कलामप्यसुरान्तकस्य प्रकाशयन्तीमवतारमन्यम् ।
अचञ्चलश्रीतटिदभ्रलेखां श्रीवत्समुद्रामुरसा दधानम् ।।२९।।

He bore the hairy sign of *śrīvatsa* on his breast which suggested that he was the incarnation of Viṣṇu, and constant prosperity would mark his life. His forehead was adorned with a circle of hair between the eyebrows. (29)

ऊर्णासनाथायतफालपट्टमुन्निद्रपद्मच्छददीर्घनेत्रम् ।
ताम्राधरोष्ठं समतुङ्गनासं मुग्धस्मिताङ्कं मुखमुद्वहन्तम् ।।३०।।
(षड्भिः कुलकम्।)

His eyes were large like the petals of blooming lotus.His nose was lofty and a sweet smile played on his red lips. Overall the child's face was surpassingly beautiful. (30)

अव्याजसौन्दर्यगुणाभिरामं कुमारमालोकयतश्चिराय ।
नृपस्य निष्पन्ददृशो मुहूर्तमानन्दबाष्पोऽभवदन्तरायः ।।३१।।

Tears of joy for a while acted as a check on the resolute look of his eyes that feasted on the blessed form of the child. (31)

आश्लिष्यतस्तस्य दृशा तनूजमन्तः प्रहर्षेण विजृम्भितेन ।
प्रायः प्रणुन्नैर्बहिरङ्गकेभ्यः प्रादुर्बभूवे पुलकप्ररोहैः ।।३२।।

The king cuddled the child with his eyes and the excessive emotion in his mind burst out as horripilation. (32)

ततः प्रतीतेऽह्नि पुरोहितेन नरेन्द्रसूनुः कृतजातकर्मा ।
समिद्धतेजाः समतामयासीन्मन्त्रप्रणीतेन मखानलेन ।।३३।।

On an auspicious day the *jāta-karma* rites of the child were performed as directed by the priest and the child grew in splendour like the god of fire that observed those rites. (33)

आकम्पयिष्यत्ययमेकवीरः संग्रामरङ्गे सकलानरातीन् ।
इत्येव निश्चित्य स दीर्घदर्शी नाम्ना सुतं कम्पन इत्यकार्षीत् ।।३४।।

The king who constantly looked ahead named his child Kampana as he clearly foresaw in his mind that in proper time the latter would become a matchless warrior. And was sure to make his enemies shaken with fear in the battle field. (34)

धात्रीभिराप्ताभिरमुं कुमारमवर्वयद् भूपतिरादरेण ।
यज्वा यथाज्याहुतिभिर्हुताशं सस्यं यथा वृष्टिभिरम्बुवाहः ।।३५।।

Just as the sacrifice tends the fire with ghee offerings and just as the cloud upholds the corn with rains so too the king had his child brought up by reliable maids. (35)

क्रमेण धात्रीजनशिक्षितानि वचांसि यातानि च मन्थराणि ।
स्खलत्पदान्यस्य धराधिनाथो निशम्य दृष्ट्वा च स निर्वृतोऽभूत् ।।३६।।

He was overjoyed to hear the lisping words and look at the tottering gaits of his child who had his lessons on talking and walking from his foster mother. (36)

तदाननं तस्य सुगन्धि जिघ्रन्नालक्ष्यदन्ताङ्कुरदर्शनीयम् ।
न तृप्तिमासादयति स्म राजा नवोदयं हंस इवारविन्दम् ।।३७।।

Like a swan that ever loves the touch of budding lotuses the king was never satisfied with kissing the fragrant mouth of his child with no teeth yet manifest in it. (37)

तथा न कर्पूरभरैर्न हारैर्न चन्दनैर्नाप्यमृतांशुपादैः ।
यथाभवन्निर्वृतमस्य गात्रं सुताङ्गसंस्पर्शभुवा सुखेन ।।३८।।

The enjoyable feeling which the king had while embracing the cherub boy was not to be matched by the contact of camphor, pearl, sandal paste or moon beams. (38)

कलक्वणत्काञ्चनकिङ्किणीकं गृहाङ्गणे जानुचरं कुमारम् ।
आलोकयन्तावमृताम्बुराशेर्मग्नाविवान्तः पितरावभूताम् ।।३९।।

The king and the queen felt themselves bathed in ocean of nectar as they enjoyed looking at their child crawling on his knees on the floor of the palace, with the small bells tinkling in his ornaments. (39)

अथ क्रमात् पार्थिवधर्मपत्नी सुतावुभौ **कम्पनसङ्गमाख्यौ** ।
असूत चिन्तामणिपारिजातौ पयःपयोधेरिव वीचिरेखा ।।४०।।

Then in course of time the queen bore to the king two other sons called Kampana and Saṅgama who were like *pārijāta* and *cintāmaṇi* that sprang from the milky ocean. (40)

स राजसूनुः सह सोदराभ्यां [दिने दिने वृद्धिमुपाससाद ।
शशीव सानन्दमुदीक्ष्यमाणः प्रजाभिरालोकसमुत्सुकाभिः ।।४१।।]

The prince along with his two brothers began to grow day by day and people were in elation when they looked at him like looking at the waxing moon. (41)

पशुपतिरिव नेत्रैः सोमसूर्याग्निरूपै-
र्नय इव निरपायैः प्राभवोत्साहमन्त्रैः ।
भव इव पुरुषार्थैर्धर्मकामार्थसंज्ञै-
स्त्रिभिरपि नरपालस्तैस्तनूजैरभासीत् ।।४२।।

The king with his three children shine like Śiva with his three eyes – the moon, the sun and the fire – or like statesmanship with its three consistent aspects – power, courage and counsel – or like life with its three ends – virtue, wealth and enjoyment. (42)

।। इति श्रीगङ्गादेव्या विरचिते मधुराविजयम्-
नाम्नि [वीर*] कम्परायचरिते द्वितीयः सर्गः ।।

Thus ends the second canto, of the life of Vīra Kamparāya known as *Madhurāvijayam* composed by Śrī Gaṅgādevī.

तृतीयः सर्गः

Canto 3

ततो यथावत्कृतचौलसत्क्रियो नरेन्द्रसूनुः स्वत एव लब्धवान् ।
कलासु शश्वत् सकलासु कौशलं गुरूपदेशस्त्वपदेशतामगात् ।।१।।

After the tonsure ceremony, the prince became proficient in all the arts without any external assistance, and in his case training by teachers was more or less a superfluity. (1)

स तीर्थलब्धायुधशस्त्रसंविदा गुणाभिरामो गुरुणैव शिक्षितः ।
शरासनासिप्रमुखेषु शातवीरगच्छदस्त्रेष्वखिलेषु पाटवम् ।।२।।

He was trained in military science by his own father who had attained its secrets from an excellent master. Thus coached under him, he became a master in exerting the bow and the sword and in the use of all phenomenal arms. (2)

स सत्यवाग् भूरिबलो धनुर्धरस्तुरङ्गमारोहणकर्ममर्मवित् ।
कृपाणविद्यानिपुणः पृथाभुवामदर्शि संङ्घात इवैकतां गतः ।।३।।

He spoke the truth, had massive body strength and was an authority in handling the bow, he was a fine horseman and a master in sword play, he possessed all the expertise that each of the five Pāṇḍavas was known for. (3)

स पञ्चबाणद्विपकेलिदीर्घिकां धरानुरागद्रुमपुष्पमञ्जरीम्(?) ।
नितम्बिनीनेत्रचकोरचन्द्रिकाभवापदास्कन्दितशैशवां दशाम् ।।४।।

He reached his youthhood which could be described as the sporting lake of the elephant Manmatha, as the bunch of flowers called love, as the moonlight for the *cakora* birds called women's eyes. (4)

स नव्यतारुण्यनिरस्तशैशवो विभुर्विभक्तावयवो व्यराजत ।
वसन्तनिर्धूततुषारमण्डलः पतिर्दिनानामिव तीव्रदीधितः ।।५।।

His body shone markedly in its full shape, now that boyhood

had entirely passed away and youthhood had emphasized itself, like the sun shines in his total brilliance after the passing away of the dewy season. (5)

स सर्वतः पर्वतकन्दराश्रयैः परिग्रहानुग्रहकाङ्क्षिभिर्गजैः ।
वितीर्णमुत्कोचतयेव धीरधीरधारयद् विभ्रममन्धरं गतम् ।।६।।

His walking was elegant and stately. It was like the elephants house in the mountain cave catching them to gift them and kept by him – that is a favour for which they (receivers) always longed for. (6)

स रूपगर्वेण निरास्थदङ्घ्रिणा स्मरस्य नूनं जयवैजयन्तिकाम् ।
न चेत् कथं तस्य तलेऽतिकोमले सुलेखमालक्ष्यत मीनलाञ्छनम् ।।७।।

In his extremely beautiful palm of hands there was the auspicious fish mark. Why should such a mark emerge there unless it be that Kāma had capitulated his fish banner by way of accepting his defeat by the beauty of the prince's feet? (7)

शुभाकृतेस्तस्य सुवर्णमेखलं कटिस्थलं स्थूलशिलाविशङ्कटम् ।
व्यडम्बयन्नूतनधातुपट्टिकापरिष्कृतामञ्जनभूभृतस्तटीम् ।।८।।

The loins of the beautiful prince, hard as stone with their golden hand, resembled the base of the Añjana hill surrounded by a fresh streak of red-coloured mineral. (8)

अधारयद् दर्शितदेहसौष्ठवां स राजसूनुस्तनुवृत्तमध्य(मा?ता)म् ।
पराक्रमत्रासितचित्तवृत्तिभिर्मृगाधिराजैरुपदीकृतामिव ।।९।।

His waist shapely and slender, which greatly enhanced the beauty of his person, suggested the idea of the lions having yielded their domination, as they were extremely afraid of his strength. (9)

व्यराजतोरःस्थलमस्य तावता विशालभावेन कवाटबन्धुरम् ।
करीन्द्रकुम्भप्रतिमं मृगीदृशां कुचद्वयं याति न यावता बहिः ।।१०।।

His panel like chest was just so expansive as to be able to hold in its vastness the breasts of beautiful womens which can well match up to the frontal globes of an elephant's head. (10)

घनांसपीठौ कठिनारुणाङ्गुली पटुप्रकोष्ठौ परिघानुकारिणौ ।
महौजसस्तस्य मनोहरौ भुजावपश्यदाजानुविलम्बिनौ जनः ॥११॥

His beam-like hands with strong reddish fingers at their end hung up to his knees. They were attractive and immensely powerful. Springing as they did from his heavy shoulders, they were always a lovely sight for the people to see. (11)

विहाय मध्यं यदि लक्ष्मरेखया बहिः प्रसार्येत सुधांशुमण्डलम् ।
दरोदितश्मश्रु(धृ?कृ)तश्रियस्तदा तदाननेन्दोरुपमानतां व्रजेत् ॥१२॥

If the black spot in the moon could be removed from its place in the centre and drawn as a line at the edge of her sphere, then it might be likened to his face, with the beard just making its appearance. (12)

विनिद्रपङ्केरुहदामदीर्घयोर्दृशोरुपान्ते जनितोऽस्य शोणिमा ।
अनर्गलस्वप्रसरप्ररोधकश्रुतिद्वयीदर्शितरोषयोरिव ॥१३॥

The redness that appeared in the corner of his lotus-like eyes suggested anger against the ears that set a limit to the freedom of their expansive eyes. (13)

अनुल्बणामायततुङ्गबन्धुराममस्त लोकः स्फुटमस्य नासिकाम् ।
विशृङ्खलव्याप्लुवदीक्षणद्वयीपरस्पराक्रान्तिनिवारणार्गलाम् ॥१४॥

The world thought of his long and lofty nose as a demarcating line that prohibited each one of the eyes from interfering on the zone of each other. (14)

अधारयद् गर्भितरक्तसन्ध्यकं नृपात्मजः केशकलापमायतम् ।
दृढानुरागच्छुरितैर्मृगीदृशामनुप्रविष्टं हृदयैरिवान्तरा ॥१५॥

The prince had his long tuft of hair dressed with red blossoms which looked like emblems expressing lovelorned hearts of beautiful women. (15)

सह प्रतापेन समुन्नतिं वपुर्वलर्क्षभावं यशसा विलोचने ।
गुणैः परीणाहममुष्य कन्धरा स्वरेण गाम्भीर्यमगच्छदाशयः ।।१६।।

His body and prowess grew side by side. Also side by side his eyes and fame became more and more white coloured. His neck, along with his qualities extended progressively more and more so both his mind and voice together gained profundity. (16)

अथैनमासादितयौवनोदयं नरेन्द्रकन्याभिरयोजयन्नृपः ।
धनागमः संभृतरत्नसंपदं वरापगाभिर्निधिमम्मसामिव ।।१७।।

The king, seeing that the prince had attained his youthhood, married him to several princesses, and the unions shared the magnificence of the ocean receiving the rivers at the beginning of the rainy season. (17)

शचीव शक्रस्य रमेव शार्ङ्गिणः सतीव शम्भो........... ।
.... ।।१८।।

Like Śacī to Śakra (Indra), Ramā (Lakṣmī) to Śārṅgin (Viṣṇu) and Satī (Pārvatī) to Śambhū (Śiva). (18)

[नरेन्द्रसूनुर्नयनाभिरामया तया समं निर्विशति स्म सुभ्रुवा ।
परस्परप्रेमरसोत्तरं सुखं दिवौकसामप्यतिमात्रदुर्लभम् ।।१९।।

The prince enjoyed marital happiness with the beautiful-looking princesses. They loved each other so well and their happiness was so ideal that even the gods felt jealous. (19)

अरातिवर्गोन्मयनेन विश्रुतं विधातुमत्यन्तविनीतमप्यमुम् ।
कदाचिदर्थोल्लसितेन भूपतिः स वाङ्मयेनैवमुपादिशत् सुतम् ।।२०।।

Perfectly disciplined as the prince was, the king one day wishing to make him famous by the conquest of the enemies began to give him important words of counsel. (20)

धियः प्रकाशादुपदेशसंभृतात् तमो हि तारुण्यविजृम्भितं जनाः ।
समुज्झितुं तात! भवन्ति पारितास्तदे*] तदाकर्णयितुं त्वमर्हसि ।।२१।।

A darkness always swarms youthful age, and wise men have found out that only the lamp of cleverness lighted by proper advice is able to dispel it. So it acts you to lend me your ears and listen to what I am about to say. (21)

गुरूपदेशः किल कथ्यते बुधैरकर्कशं किंचन रत्नकुण्डलम् ।
अमेचकं नूतनमञ्जनं सतामजातगात्रक्षयमद्भुतं तपः ॥२२॥

Wise men consider training imparted by a *guru*, as a jewelled earring lacking hardness, potent ointment without colour, and a magnificent form of sacrament involving no-self mortification. (22)

मुहुः प्रसर्पन्मदमीलितेक्षणाः क्षणाधिरोहद्रजसो मलीमसाः ।
गजा इव स्तम्भनिरुद्धचेतसः खला न गृह्णन्ति नियन्तृचोदितम् ॥२३॥

Unvirtuous people do not mind the promptings of good leaders. They close their eyes in their intoxication. They are unclean because of the dust of sin they raise against themselves. They close themselves to deep injustice. In all this deeds they resemble elephants in rut. (23)

मदान्धकारो हि महानिशीथिनी प्रबोधचन्द्रप्रतिरोधकालिका ।
मनोजमत्तद्विपवैजयन्तिका शरीरिणां शश्वदलङ्घिनी दशा ॥२४॥

The darkness of intoxication such as of youthhood is akin to that of a starless night. Nothing like moonlight excitement during its sway. It marks the triumph of sexual passion and is a bad period of life not easy to overcome by one in personified state. (24)

भवत्यहंकारमहीरुहाङ्कुरे दयापयश्शोषणदारुणोष्मणि ।
तमःप्रदोषे तरुणिम्नि कस्य वा समञ्जसं पश्यति दृष्टिरञ्जसा ॥२५॥

When the tree of selfishness puts forth its shoots, it dries up the springs of mercy. The beginning of youthhood is really like the fading of light from the mind and how can one have anything like proper observation at such a dark hour. (25)

युवानमज्ञातनयागमक्रमं स्वतन्त्रमैश्वर्यमदोद्धतं नृपम् ।
विपत् क्षणेन व्यसनानुबन्धजा क्षिणोति चन्द्रं क्षणदेव तामसी ।।२६।।

Youth destitute of judgement, and rulers unsighted by affluence, going in their own way, soon become the favourites of danger which overtakes them as a night of eclipse of full moon. (26)

अशेषदोषाङ्कुरकुञ्जभूमयो मदान्धचेतोमृगबन्धवागुराः ।
कथं नु विश्वासपदं मनीषिणां मनोजमायाभटशस्त्रिकाः स्त्रियः ।।२७।।

Which wise man would trust women who are the abode of all shortcomings and who are like nets entangle the mind resembling the leaping blind deer? (27)

फलोत्तरा भूमिरनत्ययं बलं महार्हरत्नाभरणं च संपदः ।
किमन्यदात्मा च कलत्रपुत्रकैः परार्थमेव ध्रुवमक्षदेविनः ।।२८।।

Even if a gambler has all wealth like fruitful earth, valuable ornaments, riches and even his own body, his strength, his wives and his sons do not belong to him, but belong to others. (28)

विना फलं जीवितसंशयप्रदां विनोदबुद्ध्या मृगयां भजेत कः ।
प्रमाद्यतां पार्थिवान्धहस्तिनामियं हि वारी कथिता विचक्षणैः ।।२९।।

Which wise man will indulge in hunting wild beasts threatening his own life? Those that know characterize it as a bottomless pit into which kings, like elephants in rut fall, into the careless situation. (29)

समग्रतारुण्यमदस्य संपदा स्खलद्गतेर्यन्मदिरानिषेवणम् ।
स एष दोषत्रयजे महाज्वरे ग्रहाभिभूतस्य भुजङ्गनिग्रहः ।।३०।।

When the intoxication of youthhood is on, when wealth is making one waver at every step, who could not think of getting into the habit of drinking. It would be like getting a bad complication in fever. (30)

हितानि कुर्वन्नपि नानुरक्तये जनस्य जल्पन् परुषं रुषा नृपः ।
पयांसि वर्षन्नपि किं न भीषणः कठोरविस्फूर्जथुगर्जितो घनः ॥३१॥

However much you may be committed to doing good, esteem could never be gained if you are in the habit of replete into insensitive words. A cloud may give welcome showers, but at the same time, will be frightened by its lightning and thunder. (31)

दुनोति दण्डेन दुरुत्सहेन यः प्रसह्य राष्ट्रं पदमात्मसंपदाम् ।
स वृक्षमारुह्य कुठारपातनं करोति मूलोद्दलनाय दुर्मतिः ॥३२॥

Subjects are the wealth of kings. When that is so, who could think of impose fear on them by implementing vicious punishments? Nobody would go up a tree and put the axe to its roots. (32)

मदादपात्रेषु ददाति मन्दधीर्धनानि धर्मादिकसाधनानि यः ।
निपात्यते तेन मखक्रियोचितं हविश्चितासद्मनि कृष्णवर्त्मनि ॥३३॥

An idiot who, in unawareness throws away wealth as gifts to the undeserving, wealth which is indispensable for the upkeep of *dharma*, really heaves in oblations that deserve to be used in holy sacrifices, otherwise it is like putting them to the fire that which consumes lifeless body. (33)

अथैभिरैश्वर्यशरीरयक्ष्मभिर्हताखिलाङ्गैर्व्यसनैरुपद्रुताः ।
तमःपराभूतनिजौजसो नृपाः प्रयान्ति कालाद् द्विषतामुपेक्ष्यताम् ॥३४॥

Monarchs ridden with ignorance should overcome by these vices, which are like consumption of food which enter into body politics which become in course of time – become in course of time objects of disrespect to their enemies. (34)

उपेयुषीं पुण्यवशेन संपदं गुणानुरोधादुपभोक्तुभक्षमाः ।
स्वचापलेन श्लथयन्ति दुर्धियो वलीमुखाः पुष्पमयीमिव स्रजम् ॥३५॥

Fools, who are not able to protect their good qualities and wealth got by them on account of merits in previous birth are to be like the monkeys in whose hands a garland of flowers has been given. The former, like the latter in their unbalanced state, know only to destroy what they have been given. (35)

भवादृशास्तु स्वत एव शुद्धया गुरूपदेशैर्गुणितप्रकाशया ।
धिया निरस्तव्यसनानुबन्धया विलोक्य कार्याणि विधातुमीशते ।।३६।।

But youth like you who have their intellect appropriately shaped and cleansed by the training of established *guru*s know how to keep away from vices and always behave in the proper manner. (36)

तदेवमात्मन्यवधार्य धैर्यतस्तथा विधेयं भवतापि धीमता ।
यथेयमेकान्तचला भवद्गुणैर्लभेत लक्ष्मीः स्थिरतामनारतम् ।।३७।।

Therefore, to have to take courage in both hands and intensely consider the pros and cons of everything and act in such a way that the goddesses of prosperity, infamous for her fickle mind, does not turn aside from you even for a moment. (37)

क्रमागताः कर्मकृतो विमत्सरास्तरस्विनस्तापितवैरिमानसाः ।
महीभुजस्त्यक्तमदा मदाज्ञया तवान्तिके तात! वसन्ति साम्प्रतम् ।।३८।।

Rulers of earth, who are men of action, and my hereditary friends, in whose heart no malice dwells, and who, though unostentatious, are famed in suppressing disloyal state of minds are now, camping near you hear or listen by this it is my order, my dear son! (38)

सहस्रशस्तुङ्गतुरङ्गवीचयो मदद्विपद्वीपविशेषितान्तराः ।
भवन्तमुग्रायुधनक्रराजयो भजन्ति नित्यं बहला बलाब्धयः ।।३९।।

You know, you are encircled now by an ocean-like army. Horses in thousands act as its waves, elephants in rut appear in the midst like huge islands, and destructive weapons like sharks abound in its waters. (39)

तदेवमुज्जृम्भितभूरिपौरुषः पराक्रमं वैरिषु कर्तुमर्हसि ।
उपप्लुताशेषजगत्सु रोषणो वृषेव शातां शतकोटिमद्रिषु ।।४०।।

So, I would ask you to exhibit your manliness and ever-increasing prowess and strike at your enemies and subdue them, even as the lord of the gods (Indra) did in the case of the (winged) mountains enraged at their efforts to destroy the world. (40)

उपेत्य तुण्डीरमखण्डितोद्यमः प्रमथ्य **चम्प**प्रसुखान् रणोन्मुखान् ।
प्रशाधि **काञ्ची**मनुवर्तितप्रजः पतिर्निधीनामलकापुरीमिव ।।४१।।

So you better march successfully to Tuṇḍīra (Toṇḍaimaṇḍalam) and overcome the people headed by the Campa (Śambhuvarāya) who are preparing for war. Then establish yourself at Kāñcī and rule there, with due regard to the wishes of the people even like the lord of wealth (Kubera) does in the city of Alakā. (41)

अथाभिभूताखिलवन्य**भूभृतस्तुरुष्क**भङ्गस्तव नैव दुष्करः ।
निगीर्णशाखाशतसं(वृतः?हृतिः)कथं तरुप्रकाण्डं न दहेद् दवानलः ।।४२।।

Then if you subdue all the Vanya kings it would be easy for you to break the power of the Turuṣkas. Would it be difficult for the fire that had consumed with its flames hundreds of branches of a tree, to destroy the trunk? (42)

अनेन **देशानधिकृत्य दक्षिणान्** वितन्यते राक्षसराजदुर्नयः ।
त्वयापि लोकत्रयतापहारिणा विधीयतां राघवकर्म निर्मलम् ।।४३।।

This Turuṣkas is acting like Rāvaṇa in regard to the southern kingdoms. If you play the part praiseworthy of Śrī Rāma in reducing him you will be rendering a service to the world and relieve sufferings. (43)

इतीरयित्वा विरते नरेश्वरे प्रवृष्टपाथोधरसाम्यधारिणि ।
कृतप्रणामः शिरसा प्रतीष्टवान् गुरूपदेशं गुणिनां पुरस्सरः ।।४४।।

Having delivered this speech, the king stopped, like the cloud after pouring down its watery contents becomes calm. The prince bowed low, and took to heart, like the good son he was, the advice of his father. (44)

ततो महार्हैर्गुरुणा विभूषणैः प्रसाधितः स्वावयवावतारितैः ।
परेऽपि निर्धारितजैत्रनिर्गमो निजाधिवासं प्रमनाः समासदत् ।।४५।।

Then the king took off invaluable ornaments from his own person and adorned the prince that the latter should start on his victorious expedition on the next day, he retired to his own apartments in a jubilant disposition. (45)

अथोरगाणामधिपाय भाविनं भुवो भरस्यापगमं दिनेश्वरः ।
निवेदयिष्यन्निव गाढरंहसा रथेन पातालगुहामगाहत ।।४६।।

The sun, as if anxious to inform the serpent king who bore this earth (Śeṣa) that his burden would soon be lightened, sank in haste into the subsequent area. (46)

अथ नृपसुतः सान्ध्यं निर्माय कर्म सभां गतः
क्षणमिव गुरोराज्ञां राज्ञां गणाय निवेद्य सः ।
विमतविजयव्यग्रोत्साहान् विहाय गृहाय ता-
नरमत सुखी शय्यागेहे सरोजमुखीसखः ।।४७।।

The prince, after finishing his daily worship of the *sandhyā*, and after acquainting his eager attendants with the commands of his father and dismissing them, entered his private apartments to enjoy the company of his beautiful princesses. (47)

।। इति [श्रीगङ्गादेव्या विरचिते मधुराविजयम्-
नाम्नि वीरकम्परायचरिते*] तृतीयः सर्गः ।।

Thus ends the third canto, of the life of Vīra Kamparāya known as *Madhurāvijayam* composed by Śrī Gaṅgādevī.

चतुर्थः सर्गः

Canto 4

अन्येद्युरथ राजीववनजीवनदायिनि ।
लोकैकदीपे भगवत्युदिते भानुमालिनि ।।१।।

When the divine sun, the unequalled lamp of universe, the sustainer of lotuses, born the next day, the prince woke up from his sleep. (1)

विहाय निद्रां विधिवन्निर्मिताहर्मुखक्रियः ।
आदिक्षत् पृतनाध्यक्षान् सेनासन्नहनाय सः ।।२।।

After duly performing the morning rituals of worship, ordered his generals to get the army ready for marching. (2)

अथ मन्दरसंघट्टक्षोभिताम्भोधिमण्डलः ।
रराण कोणाभिहतो रणनिर्याणदुन्दुभिः ।।३।।

Then like the clamour of the ocean, churned with the mountain of Mandāra, the reverberations of war drums beaten by drumsticks occurred at the commencement of the march. (3)

कल्पान्तोद्भ्रान्तचण्डीशडमरुध्वानडामरः ।
उदजृम्भत गम्भीरो वियदध्वनि तद्ध्वनिः ।।४।।

The sound grew louder and louder, and filled the skies as if it originated from Caṇḍīśa's *ḍamaru* (drum) beaten at the time of the great flood. (4)

प्रायो भयद्रुतामित्रपदविध्वंसनोत्सुकः ।
स जगाहे प्रतिध्वाननिभादवनिभृद्गुहाः ।।५।।

It raised echos from the caves in the mountains as if to scare the fear-ridden enemies who might otherwise take shelter in them. (5)

तस्मिन् विसर्पति त्रारामीलिताशेषलोचनः ।
शेषो युगपदज्ञासीदान्ध्यबाधिर्ययोर्दशाम् ।।६।।

As the uproar entered the inward of earth Śeṣa closed his eyes (which were also his ears), and he became blind and deaf by an only act. (6)

आबद्धकुथमातङ्गमात्तपर्याणसैन्धवम् ।
संवर्मितभटं सद्यः समनह्यत तद्बलम् ॥७॥

The army at once got ready with each of its units, viz. elephants, horses and foot soldiers, suitably covered and dressed elephants, with carpets on their back, horses fully caparisoned and riders protected in their mailed coats. (7)

विशङ्कटकटाघाटविगलन्मदनिर्झराः ।
परश्शतं जघटिरे विकटाः करिणां घटाः ॥८॥

There assembled hundreds of terrible war-elephants with ichor flowing from their wide temples. (8)

समीरणरयोदग्रा वल्गन्तः फेनिलैर्मुखैः ।
तुरङ्गाः सैन्यजलधेस्तरङ्गा इव रेजिरे ॥९॥

Horses with frothing mouths, and swift as wind were seen leaping like waves in the army-ocean. (9)

कृपाणकर्पणप्रासकुन्तकोदण्डपाणयः ।
समगच्छन्त सहसा नैकदेश्याः पदातयः ॥१०॥

There hosts of footmen assembled in no time, from different countries, armed with swords, daggers lances and bows. (10)

प्रस्थानोचितमाकल्पं बिभ्राणा बाहुशालिनः ।
राजन्यास्तोरणाभ्यर्णे नृपालं प्रत्यपालयन् ॥११॥

Wearing suitable ornaments, kings, renowned for the might of their arms, waited near the outer gate for the arrival of their overlord. (11)

सेनासरित्सिताम्भोजैर्जयश्रीकेलिदर्पणैः ।
अस्तावकाशमाकाशमातपत्रैरजायत ॥१२॥

The sky was completely filled with open umbrellas, resembling white lotuses in the river of the army, and also looking like the playing mirrors of the Goddess of Victory. (12)

विजृम्भमाणे प्रस्थानशारदारम्भसंभ्रमे ।
नृपाणां चामरालीभिर्मरालीभिरभूयत ॥१३॥

Thus the time of the march can be compared to the beginning of the autumnal season, the fly whisks waving by the side of kings appeared like swans hovering around. (13)

नृपमौलिमणिच्छायामञ्जरीपुञ्जरञ्जिताः ।
अत्याक्षुरौरसीं रक्तिं न जातु रविरश्मयः ॥१४॥

The rays of the sun never left his natural redness, as the colour of the glowing gems set in royal crowns, as beautiful as clusters of flowers, was endlessly mixing with the sunrays appeared lovely. (14)

उत्तुङ्गैर्ध्वजसंघातैर्निरुद्धे गगनाध्वनि ।
निनाय कृच्छ्रात् पातङ्गं शताङ्गं गरुडाग्रजः ॥१५॥

As the passage of the sky was entirely blocked by the flying flags in the air, Aruṇa (elder brother of Garuḍa) experienced much difficulty in driving the chariot of the sun across. (15)

पोषितो हयहेषाभिर्बृंहितो गजबृंहितैः ।
वर्धितस्तूर्यनिध्वानैः कोऽपि कोलाहलोऽभवत् ॥१६॥

Nourished by the neighing of the horses, intensified by the loud trumpeting of the elephants and extended by the sound of the instruments of war music (war drums) the noise that born was something unbelievable. (16)

ततो धृतसमायोगः समयज्ञो महीपतिः ।
हितैः पुरोहितैर्यात्रामुहूर्तं प्रत्यवैक्षत ॥१७॥

The king who had himself the knowledge of the proper time, however awaited with his followers, for the formal fixing of the auspicious moment by his loyal priests. (17)

तमसूचयदाप्तेभ्यो दक्षिणं दक्षिणो भुजः ।
स्फुरितैर्भाविवीरश्रीपरिरम्भमहोत्सवम् ॥१८॥

His throbbing right hand foretold the propitious moments of the forthcoming embrace by the Goddess of Valour, ahead of everyone else. (18)

अथर्ववेदिनो विप्रास्तं विशेषैर्जयाशिषाम् ।
अवर्धयन् मन्त्रपूतैर्हविर्भिरिव पावकम् ॥१९॥

Brāhmaṇas chanting the *Atharvaveda* augmented the chances of his victory with their (hearty) blessings just as the sacrificial fire is made to glow by oblations sanctified by hymns. (19)

अथ निर्गत्य भवनादवैक्ष्यत महीक्षिता ।
धारितस्तोरणाभ्यर्णे तुङ्गस्तुरगपुङ्गवः ॥२०॥

The king now came out of his palace and had a good look at his tall swift horse saddled in readiness near the outer gate. (20)

सपक्ष इव तार्क्ष्यस्य सजातिरिव चेतसः ।
सखेव गन्धवाहस्य संघात इव रंहसः ॥२१॥

Like a friend of Garuḍa, like the next of kin of the mind, and like a friend of Vāyu, the swift animal looked like speed itself in its collection. (21)

अपर्याप्तामतिक्रान्तचेतोवृत्तेः स्वरंहसः ।
विस्तारयन्निव महीं चटुलैः खुरघट्टनैः ॥२२॥

As if the horse felt that the space of the earth was insufficient for the demonstration of his great speed which was faster than even that of the mind, seemed broadened it by constantly beating his hoofs. (22)

जवाधरितजम्भारितुरङ्गभ्रमकारिणम् ।
मणिकुट्टिमसंक्रान्तमाक्रामन् बिम्बमात्मनः ॥२३॥

Excelling the horse of (Indra) in speed, he appeared to be attacking his own image reflected in the crystal walls. (23)

लवणोदन्वदेकान्तलङ्घनामात्रगर्वितम् ।
हसन्निव हनूमन्तं हेषितैः फेनपाण्डरैः ।।२४।।

Horses neighing along with the white froth, seemed to ridicule at Hanumān who took great pleasure in having merely crossed the saltish ocean. (24)

मुखलीनखलीनाहिरच्छपल्ययनच्छदः ।
वपुषापि गरुत्मन्तमनुगन्तुमिवोत्सुकः ।।२५।।

With the bits of (grass) in his mouth looking like a serpent, and with the wing-like cover (on his back), sparkling with the colour of tender plants, he seemed to emulate Garuḍa even in his bodily form. (25)

लोलवालाग्रलग्नेन सेव्यमानो नभस्वता ।
रंहोरहस्यशिक्षार्थं शिष्यतामिव जग्मुषा ।।२६।।

The wind, blowing from the end of the waving tail which attended on him, was like a disciple taking secret lessons in speed. (26)

मुहुः स्वजवसंरोधनमितोन्नमिताननः ।
नमस्कुर्वन्निव पुरोवर्तिनीं विजयश्रियम् ।।२७।।

By frequently raising his head up, and letting it down again, to keep his swiftness in bounds he appeared to be offering salutations to the Goddess of Victory standing in front of him. (27)

खुरधूतधराधूलिस्थलीकृतनभस्स्थलः ।
वारयन्निव रथ्यानां रवेः खेचरतामदम् ।।२८।।
(नवभिः कुलकम्।)

With the heaps of dust raised by his hoofs the regions of the sky were rendered like floor and this served to give the recline direct to the claims of the sun's horses that they walked on airy tract. (28)

देहब(न्ध?द्ध)मिवोत्साहं तमारुह्य महीपतिः ।
अमंस्त पृथिवीं सर्वामात्मनो हस्तवर्तिनीम् ।।२९।।

The king mounted the horse, the embodiment of strength, and (in his elation) felt as if the entire kingdom of the earth had already passed into his hands. (29)

स तत्र तत्र संभूतैः सैन्यैः सङ्ख्यातिलाङ्घिभिः ।
अन्तर्हिततदाभोगमत्यगाद् गृहगोपुरम् ।।३०।।

With numberless troops pouring in from all directions, the king, with his visible view, crossed the outer gate. (30)

तमञ्जलिभिरानम्रकिरीटतलकीलितैः ।
प्रणेमुर्धरणीपालास्तुरङ्गस्कन्धवर्तिनः ।।३१।।

With crowns on their bent heads, with their hands folded (in reverence), the monarchs of earth saluted him, as he emerged, seated on the back of his horse. (31)

आलोकशब्दमुखरैरस्याग्रे पादचारिभिः ।
चोलकेरलपाण्ड्याद्यैर्वेत्रित्वं प्रत्यपद्यत ।।३२।।

With shouts of joy on seeing him, the Coḷa, Kerala and Pāṇḍya monarchs assumed the role of staff bearers and choose to walk in front of him. (32)

आचारलाजैः पौराणां पुरन्ध्र्यस्तनवाकिरन् ।
अम्भसां बिन्दुभिः शुभ्रैरभ्रमाला इवाचलम् ।।३३।।

Like a row of clouds raining drops of water on a mountain, the highly regarded matrons of the town, showered the customary parched grain on him. (33)

अथ **कम्प**महीपालः कम्पयन् द्विषतां मनः ।
प्रातिष्ठत दिशं भेजे मलयाचलमुद्रिताम् ।।३४।।

As he marched in state, King Kampana caused a tremble in the hearts of his rivals and turned to the direction of the quarter which had the Malaya Mountain for its boundary. (34)

स नयन् महतीं सेनां व्यरुजद् वीरकुञ्जरः ।
पयोदमालामाकर्षन् पौरस्त्य इव मारुतः ।।३५।।

Leading such a huge army, the great hero looked like the eastern wind dragging behind it a sequence of heavy clouds. (35)

रजोभिर्मुहुरु(द्भू?द्भ्रू)तैर्लघूभवति भूमरे ।
कथञ्चित् पृतनाभारं चक्षमे फणिनां पतिः ।।३६।।

The load of the earth having become lightened by heaps of dust rising up, Ādiśeṣa managed to bear the weight of the royal army. (36)

प्रतापादित्यकीर्तीन्दुयुगपद्ग्रासलालसः ।
परागः परभूपानामुपरागोऽभवन्नवः ।।३७।।

The dust that rose up acted simultaneously as an eclipse of both the sun of prowess and the moon of fame of the enemy (and thus affected a double eclipse at the same time). (37)

तस्य दिक्षु प्ररोहन्त्याः शतधा कीर्तिवीरुधः ।
वितताान रजस्स्तोमः करीषनिकरभ्रमम् ।।३८।।

The aggregate of dust caused the misapprehension of a huge dung heap capable of manuring the creepers of (Kampana's) fame that had begun to sprout out in all the quarters. (38)

पांसुस्थगनलक्षेण पलायत रविः क्वचित् ।
भावियुद्धामरीभूतवीराद्दलनशङ्कितः ।।३९।।

Under the pretext of being hidden away by the dust, the sun (in fact) fled to some unknown quarter, afraid that he might be pierced through by warriors transformed into gods in the approaching conflict. (39)

(Warriors who go to *vīra-svarga* after a heroic end may pierce the sun in their journey to that destination.)

प्रायः स्वनाशमुत्प्रेक्ष्य भाविनं रेणुसंचयः ।
रुरोध सिन्धुरेन्द्राणां मदधारासिरामुखम् ।।४०।।

As if apprehending early extinction, grains of dust entered the pores of glands of lordly elephants through which ichor was coming out. (40)

घर्मांशुकिरणग्रासात् परितप्त इवाधिकम् ।
अगाहत महाम्भोधीनवनीक्षोदसंचयः ।।४१।।

Having been subjected the wind collection of dust plunged into the great ocean, when trying to absorb the rays of the sun as it were, of the unbearable heat. (41)

वितेनिरे करेणूनां करशीकररणेवः ।
घनस्य सेनारजसः करकाकारचातुरीम् ।।४२।।

Water particles sprayed from the trunks of female elephants gave the shape of a final hail to cloud of dust raised by the marching army. (42)

ततः सेनागजेन्द्राणां कर्णतालानिलोद्धता ।
अवार्यत रजोराजिः करशीकरदुर्दिनैः ।।४३।।

Particles of dust buffed out by big war elephants by the flap of their ears were kept back by the rain of spray from the trunks of female elephants. (43)

अथ कल्पान्तसंभिन्नसप्ताम्भोनिविसन्निभम् ।
क्रमात् प्रयातुमारेमे स्फारकोलाहलं बलम् ।।४४।।

The army which looked like the grand confluence of all the seven oceans at the time of (*mahāpralaya*) the great deluge began its orderly march with a great uproar. (44)

तुरङ्गखुरकुद्दालदलितादपि भूतलात् ।
न पुनः पांसुरुत्तस्थौ महेभमावृष्टिभिः ।।४५।।

Caught up in the temples of great elephants overflowing with ichor, dust no longer raised, though the ground was continuously being busted by the hoofs of horses. (45)

तं तुङ्गभद्राकल्लोलशीकरासङ्गशीतलः ।
आनुकूल्येन यात्रार्थमाद्दकर्षेव मारुतः ।।४६।।

The cool breeze, cool by reason of its contact with fine drops of water from the waves of the Tuṅgabhadrā, authenticated the quite salutations for the onward march of the army. (46)

अथ लङ्घितकर्णाटः पञ्चपैरेव वासरैः ।
प्रापत् कम्पमहीपालः कण्टकाननपट्टणम् ।।४७।।

King Kampana reached Muḷuvayipaṭṭaṇam after crossing the Karṇāṭa country within five or six days. (47)

स तत्र दिवसान् कांश्चिदतिवाह्य महाबलः ।
अभिषणयितुं चम्पमुपाक्रमत कालवित् ।।४८।।

In that city he was bidding his time, and when the appropriate hour arrived he started to initiate his attack against the Śambhuvarāya ruler. (48)

प्रसृतैस्तच्चमूधूलिस्तोमैः क्षीरतरङ्गिणी ।
कीर्त्या चम्पक्षितीन्द्रस्य साकं कलुषतामगात् ।।४९।।

The dust raised by his army made both the Palar and the fame of the Śambhuvarāya monarch look grimy. (49)

स दुग्धवाहिनोवीचिमारुताधूतशाखिनि ।
विरिञ्चिनगराभ्यर्णे न्यवेशयदनीकिनीम् ।।५०।।

King Kampana struck camp with the army near Viriñcinagara (Viriñcipuram) where the branches of the trees were being shaken by the wind proceeding from the (waves) ripples of the Palar. (50)

अथ सन्नद्धसैन्यस्तं न्यरुन्ध द्रमिडाधिपम् ।
घनीकृतहिमानीको हेमन्त इव भास्करम् ।।५१।।

Having come in all willingness, King Kampana started to lay seige to the town of the lord of the Tamils, like the dewy spell blocking up the course of the sun with sporadic snowfall. (51)

संवर्तमारुताक्षिप्तसमुद्रद्वयसन्निभौ ।
व्यूहौ **द्रमिडकर्णाटनाथयोः** संनिपेततुः ।।५२।।

The arrayed forces of both the Karṇāṭa and the Tamil kings attacked each other, like two oceans brought against each other by stormy winds at the time of the great flood. (52)

पादातप्राप्तपादातं हास्तिकाक्रान्तहास्तिकम् ।
आश्वीयमिलिताश्वीयमासीदायोधनं तयोः ।।५३।।

The fight began to rage, foot soldiers falling on foot soldiers, elephant herds attacking elephant herds, troops of horses colliding with troops of horses. (53)

असह्यैस्तत्र वीराणां सिंहनादाविजृम्भणैः ।
दिगन्तदन्तिनो मुक्तफीट्कारं मुमुहुर्मुहुः ।।५४।।

Unable to bear the lion-like roars emanating from warriors on both sides, the elephants, of the quarters, with their trumpeting wholly silenced, almost lost their consciousness. (54)

रजस्तमसि वीरास्त्रसङ्घसंघट्टनोत्थितैः ।
बभ्रे स्फुलिङ्गसंघातैः खद्योतनिवहद्युतिः ।।५५।।

Sparks produced in large numbers by the clash of the weapons on either side bore a close likeness to a collection of glow of worms in the darkness of the dust. (55)

संग्रामदेवतापाङ्गविभ्रमभ्रान्तिदायिनः ।
मिथो धनुर्धरैर्मुक्ताः पेतुः शातमुखाः शराः ।।५६।।

Even like the fancied side glances of the amorous goddesses of fight the sharp-pointed arrows let fly against one another by bowmen fell to the ground. (56)

क्षतजार्द्राः प्रवीराणां प्रेङ्खन्त्यः खड्गलेखिकाः ।
जिघत्सतः कृतान्तस्य जिह्वा इव विरेजिरे ।।५७।।

The blood-stained sword blades waving in the hands of heroic warriors appeared like the lolling tongue of Yama eager to make a meal of them.(57)

आस्रापगासु परितो निस्सृतासु सहस्रशः ।
भटानां भल्लनिर्लूनैरम्भोजायितमाननैः ।।५८।।

In the countless rivers of blood which began to flow on all sides, the faces of soldiers cut-off by the *bhāllā* arrow looked like lotuses. (58)

कृपाणकृत्तान् वेतण्डशुण्डादण्डानिवाभितः ।
भुजङ्गशङ्किनो गृध्रा जगृहुर्भूभुजां भुजान् ।।५९।।

The arms of kings severed by swords resembled the trunks of elephants but were mistaken for snakes by the eagles that snatched them away. (59)

वेतण्डशुण्डाहर्म्याग्रमास्थिताः सचमत्क्रियम् ।
आद्रियन्त कबन्धानां (न?र)क्तं नक्तंचरस्त्रियः ।।६०।।

The blood flowing from human trunks was very much liked by the demons who deftly seated themselves on the trunks of elephants as if on split ends of places. (60)

वीराः कुञ्जरकुम्भेषु शायिनः शत्रुसायकैः ।
प्राबुध्यन्त सुरस्त्रीणां कुजकुम्भेषु तत्क्षणात् ।।६१।।

Brave fighters sent to (everlasting) sleep by enemy arrows on the protrusion of their elephants, soon woke up on the pot-like breasts of divine damsels. (61)

ततः **कम्पनरेन्द्रस्य** भटैर्भुजबलोत्कटैः ।
पलायत पराभूता **द्रमिडेन्द्र**वरूथिनी ।।६२।।

Then the army of the Tamil king routed by the mighty forces of Kampana took to flight. (62)

उल्लङ्घ्योल्लङ्घ्य धावद्भिर्भीत्या भ्रंशितमायुधम् ।
प्रायः प्रथनसंन्यासे शपथः कैश्चिदादधे ।।६३।।

Some men fleeing in great disorder let fall their weapons in great terror and swore they would never fight again. (63)

हतानुकारिणः केचित् क्षितौ निपतितास्ततः ।
क्रोष्टुर्भयेन धावन्तः **कर्णाटान्** पर्यहासयन् ।।६४।।

Others pretending death, dropped down, but fearing the presence of jackals, they at once rose up and started running pell-mell, giving delight to the Karṇāṭa forces. (64)

विक्षेप्तुं विस्मृतैश्चर्मफलकैर्निर्मितप्लवाः ।
मृषैव केचिदतरन् मृगतृष्णातरङ्गिणीः ।।६५।।

Yet others, mistaking a mirage for water (river) made futile attempts to cross it with a boat improvised out of the shields which they had forgotten to abandon (in their flight). (65)

छायामेवात्मनः केचिद् धावन्तो भीतिभाविताः ।
अरातिशङ्क्या कष्टं दष्टाङ्गुलि ववन्दिरे ।।६६।।

There were still others who in their flight mistook their own shadows for the pursuing enemy in the extremity of their fright and began to prostrate before them, biting their fingers. (66)

अथ तस्य पुरीमेव नीत्वा शिबिरतां नृपः ।
अचलं **राजगम्भीर**मरुन्ध द्विषदाश्रितम् ।।६७।।

King Kampana, then converted the Tamil kings town into an encampment for his own forces, and from there began to lay siege to the hill fortress named Rājagambhīra (Rājagambhīra-malai) in which the enemy had sought asylum. (67)

तद्दुन्दुभिप्रतिध्वानमुखरैः कन्दरामुखैः ।
भयादमन्दमाक्रन्दमकार्षीदिव पर्वतः ।।६८।।

The sound of his war drums raised echoes from every cave of the hill and it looked as if the hill itself had begun to yell out in fright. (68)

प्रवाताभिमुखाधूतैः पताकापाणिपल्लवैः ।
आरोहणाय राजेन्द्रमाजुहावेव भूधरः ।।६९।।

With flags flying in the direction of high winds, the hill (fort) gave the impression that it was greeting king (Kampana) and welcoming him with its arms (the flags) to come to its top. (69)

अथ प्रववृते युद्धं सैन्ययोरुभयोरपि ।
पतदुत्पतदस्त्रांशुज्वलितोर्वीनभस्स्थलम् ॥७०॥

Again ferocious fight commenced between the two sides, and the weapons falling down and shooting up, lit up both earth and sky by their resplendence. (70)

भ्रश्यत्तालफलाकारैः प्राकाराद् बाणपातितैः ।
रणश्रीकन्दुकभ्रान्तिर्विदधे वीरमूर्धभिः ॥७१॥

Heads severed by arrows resembled palmyra fruits as they fell down from the ramparts and caused an illusion of balls belonging to the deity of war. (71)

अग्रे निपेतुर्नृपतेर्ग्रावाणो यन्त्रविच्युताः ।
दुर्गेणातरदानार्थं दूताः संप्रेषिता इव ॥७२॥

Like messengers (tax collectors) sent by the stronghold itself claiming the tolls for the entry of the Karṇāṭa troops, the stones let down from catapults fell just in front of the king. (72)

धानुष्कमुक्तबाणाग्निज्वलितोर्ध्वगृहावलिः ।
विजयारात्रिकं तस्य मूर्ध्नेवाद्रिरधारयत् ॥७३॥

The hill, with the houses lit up by the fire from the missiles of bowmen, looked like holding lamps in readiness for the happy ceremony of *harati* to mark the auspicious victory of the king. (73)

विन्यस्तकुन्तनिश्रेणीश्रेणिभिर्न्नीरपुङ्गवैः ।
आक्रान्तसालशृङ्गाग्रेरारुह्यत महीधरः ॥७४॥

The assent of the hill was accomplished by heroic men by means of rows of lances planted as ladders and climbing up to the tops of *śāla* trees. (74)

अथोद्भटभटक्ष्वेडागलितभ्रूणगार्भिणम् ।
निहतास्रनदीमज्जज्जनताशास्यजीवितम् ।।७५।।

.... ।

अलब्धनिर्गमं दुर्गमासीदेवमुपद्रुतम् ।।७६।।
(युग्मकम् ।)

With all means (and chances) of (escape) coming out completely blocked, and stronghold was subjected to such great distress that the embryos of women, big with children, slipped out at the very sight of the fierce troops jumping in, and people immersed in the river of blood of the slain prayed for their lives. (75-76)

निर्जगाम निजागाराच्चम्पक्ष्मापोऽपि कोपनः ।
कृपाणपाणिर्वल्मीकाज्जिह्वाल इव जिह्मगः ।।७७।।

The Śambhuvarāya monarch, with drawn sword, came out of his palace in great anger, like a snake with its lolling tongue might come out of a mole hill. (77)

अहंपूर्विकया वीरेष्वभितो युद्धकाङ्क्षिषु ।
प्रत्यग्रहीन्महीपालश्चम्पं सिंह इव द्विपम् ।।७८।।

Though many a soldier of valour eagerly came forward to fight saying “let me do it”, King Kampana preferred to the face of Śambhuvarāya himself. (78)

तौ निकुञ्चितपूर्वाङ्गौ निश्चलाक्षौ कृपाणिनौ ।
उचितस्थानकावास्तां चित्रन्यस्ताविव क्षणम् ।।७९।।

With the forepart of their bodies bent and eyes fixed, the two kings, sword in hand, stood still for a moment like a picture on a piece of painting. (79)

कक्ष्याविभक्तवपुषोश्चारीभिश्चरतोस्तयोः ।
पश्यद्भिः सौष्ठवं देवैरनिमेषत्वमादृतम् ।।८०।।

The gods were thankful for the total absence of winking in

their eyes, as they were looking on with fixed gaze, the fight (of the two heroes), their bodies divided at waist. (80)

अन्तर्बिम्बित**चम्पेन्द्रा कम्पेन्द्र**स्यासिपुत्रिका ।
अप्सरोभ्यः पतिं दातुमन्तर्वत्नी किलाभवत् ॥८१॥

Kampana's sword, reflecting as it did, the image of the Śambhuvarāya monarch, looked like a pregnant daughter about to give birth to a husband for the celestial nymphs. (81)

अथ वञ्चित[तत्]खड्गप्रहारः **कम्प**भूपतिः ।
अकरोदसिना **चम्प**ममरेन्द्रपुरातिथिम् ॥८२॥

Then escaping skilfully a sword plunge, King Kampana dispatched the Śambhuvarāya (monarch) as a guest to Indra's city. (82)

इत्थं सङ्गरमूर्ध्नि **चम्प**नृपतिं नीत्वा कथाशेषतां
श्रीमान् कम्पनृपेश्वरो जनयितुः संप्राप्तवाञ्छासनम् ।
काञ्चीन्यस्तजयप्रशस्तिरमिथस्संकीर्णवर्णाश्रमं
नीत्या नित्यनिरत्ययर्द्धिरशिषत् तुण्डीरभूमण्डलम् ॥८३॥

Having thus reduced (killed) the Śambhuvarāya in the field of battle, King Kampana received the decree of his father that he should rule (the territory thus conquered). With the fame of his victory duly established in Kāñcī, he inaugurated a just and prosperous rule over Tuṇḍīramaṇḍalam destroying all confusion in castes and religious orders. (83)

॥ इति [श्रीगङ्गादेव्या विरचिते मधुराविजयम्-
नाम्नि वीर*]कम्परायचरिते चतुर्थः सर्गः ॥

Thus ends the fourth canto, of the life of Vīra Kamparāya known as *Madhurāvijayam* composed by Śrī Gaṅgādevī.

पञ्चमः सर्गः

Canto 5

अथ स तत्र महीतलमण्डने मरतकाह्वयभाजि महापुरे ।
विरचितस्थितिरप्रतिशासनं जगदशेषमरक्षदनाकुलम् ।।१।।

In the vast city called Marataka which was like an embellishment of this earth, King Kampana established himself and ruled the earth peacefully and well. (1)

अरिबलापहमाश्रितनन्दनं सुमनसां मनसः प्रियदायिनम् ।
वसुमतीमवतीर्णमिवापरं हरिममंसत तं सततं प्रजाः ।।२।।

His subjects thought that he was another embodiment of Hari that had come down to this earth, because he was so victorious, and such a beloved of gods and virtuous men. (2)

प्रथितशक्तिरवाप्तफलोदयः प्रगुणयन् पणबन्धमुखान् गुणान् ।
निपुणधीर्निरपायमुपायवित् प्रभुरभुङ्क्त नवां नयसंपदम् ।।३।।

Renowned for his ability in all places, his measures were always fruitful. He increased the scope of compromise among other devices in achieving his purpose. He was highly intelligent and diplomatic. There was something original in his statecraft, which showed he was an authentic master. (3)

असुहृदां सुहृदामिव मण्डलेष्वजनि तेन न किञ्चिदलक्षितम् ।
प्रहितचारगणेन विवस्वता प्रसृतदीधितिना भुवनेष्विव ।।४।।

Even as the sun with his bright rays reveals every object on earth, the king, by his skilled service of spies, regularly knew everything that was being done by friends and foes. (4)

करपरिग्रहमाचरित प्रभौ मृदुतरं मुदितप्रकृतिर्मही ।
विविधसस्यविशेषनिरन्तरा पुलकितेव भृशं समलक्ष्यत ।।५।।

His accomplished system of light taxation pleased his subjects in his kingdom, and earth herself showed a great satisfaction by her excellent yield of corn and other produce. (5)

द्रढिमशालिनि भोगमनोहरे कटकधारिणि दानगुणो[र्जिते*] ।
नृपतिदोष्णि निवासमुपेत्य भूरलघयत् प्रथमास्पदगौरवम् ।।६।।

Earth, by finding rest on his strong, attractive, decorated and liberal hands, lightened the burden of Śeṣa who was her prime support. (6)

नरपतेः प्रतिहारमहीं मुहुर्विजयदन्तिमदोदकपङ्किलाम् ।
क्षितिभुजां भुजभूषणघट्टनप्रसृमरो मणिरेणुरशोषयत् ।।७।।

The entrance of his palace was ever crowded with elephants, and kings waiting for meeting. Elephants made it muddy with their flowing ichors, while the kings made it dry with gem dusts falling down from ornaments broken as a result of colliding with each other. (7)

अहरहर्नृपतेः पदपीठिकातटसमुल्लिखितैरलिकस्थलैः ।
पुनरिवार्पितभाग्यमयाक्षरै रजनि वैरमुचामवनीभुजाम् ।।८।।

Every day kings that had cast off their old enmity rubbed their forehead against his royal footstool. And their resultant change of fortune suggested the idea that new letters of prosperity were written on their foreheads. (8)

मगधमालवसे(म?वु)णसिंहलद्रमिलकेरलगौ(ल?ड)मुखैर्नृपैः ।
अवसराप्तिपरैरनुवासरं रुरुधिरे प्रतिहारभुवः प्रभोः ।।९।।

The royal entrance was always overwhelmed by crowds of kings, such as of Magadha, Mālava, Sevuṇa, Siṁhala, Dramila, Kerala and Gauḍa, waiting for an occasion to pay their homage. (9)

परिसरद्वयचामरधारिणीकनककङ्कणरिङ्खणनिस्वनः ।
अशमयन्नृपतेर्बिरुदावलीमुखरमागधमण्डलवैखरीम् ।।१०।।

On both sides beautiful damsels waved the *caurī* and in the jingle of their golden bracelets, the voice of court bards singing accolades was almost sunk. (10)

चतुरचङ्क्रमचारुसरस्वतीचरणनूपुरशिञ्जितमञ्जुलैः ।
भृशमरज्यत **कम्पम**हीपतिः सदसि सत्कविसूक्तिसुधारसैः ॥११॥

Kampana loved very much to listen to compositions which were sweet like the sounding of Sarasvatī's anklets as she practised graceful walking. (11)

तरलिताङ्गुलिताडितवल्लकीनिरततानिरन्तरितैः स्वरैः ।
जगुरमुष्य जगत्प्रथितं यशो गमकभङ्गितरङ्गितमङ्गनाः ॥१२॥

The ladies of the court played on the lute with their slender fingers, singing songs that told his universal acts of splendour. Sweet notes of *gamaka* that floated from the music made it most beautiful. (12)

उचिततालमुदञ्चितविभ्रमं चतुरचारिचमत्कृतसौष्ठवम् ।
मुहुरसाववरोधमृगीदृशां मुखरसोज्ज्वलमैक्षत नर्तनम् ॥१३॥

Very often the ladies of his harem entertained the king with dancing, perfect in every respect, beating time, making gestures and movements. (13)

हततरक्षु परिक्षतसैरिभं मृदितरङ्कु निषूदितसूकरम् ।
ग्लपितखड्गि गृहीतमतङ्गजं वनमसौ मृगयासु मुहुर्व्यधात् ॥१४॥

In his hunting expeditions, the king cleared the forest by killing hyenas, wounding buffaloes, scattering deer and slaughtering wild boars. He also subdued Rhinoceroses and caught elephants. (14)

अथ सुगन्धिहिमान् व्यजनानिलान् मृगदृशः कृतचन्दनचर्चिकाः ।
शशिमतीश्च निशाः प्रियतां नयन् नरपतेरुदभूद् ऋतुरूष्मलः ॥१५॥

Then summer set in. It made women have recourse to scented snows, fans and sandal. They also loved moonlit nights. (15)

विकचपाटलगन्धिसमीरणैः सलिलकेलिपरायणयौवतैः ।
रजनिदैर्ध्यहरैरधिकोल्लसद्रविमहोभिरहोभिरभूयत ॥१६॥

Days were bright and long with sunshine, and nights were

short; young women loved to enjoy water sports. Gentle winds blew, with the fragrance of the smell of full-bloomed *pāṭala* flowers. (16)

नियतिनिर्मितदक्षिणदिग्वधूविरहतापहनिवारणवाञ्छया ।
अहिमभानुरहन्यहनि ध्रुवं हरितमाप हिमाचलशीतलाम् ।।१७।।

By the verdict of eternal law, the sun had to leave the southern region, in order to obtain, as it were the cooling influence of the snow-covered Himalayas. (17)

परुषतापविशेषपरिस्खलद्रथतुरङ्गममन्दगताविव ।
अहिमधाम्नि रथाङ्गसुखावहामहरगा[हत दै*]र्ध्यवतीं दशाम् ।।१८।।

For the pleasure of the *cakravāka* birds, the days became longer and longer. In the intolerable heat of summer, it seemed that even the horses of the sun stumbled and had to move with less speed. (18)

सरसचन्दनधारिषु मौक्तिकत्रिसरनिर्झरहारिषु सुभ्रुवाम् ।
कुचतटेषु निदाघनिपीडितो धृतिमघात् कुसुमायुधकुञ्जरः ।।१९।।

The elephant cupid, getting scorched in the sun, found shelter in the breasts of beautiful ladies, which were wet with pastes of sandal and had the cooling touch of pearl strings. (19)

सलिलकेलिकुतूहलकुन्तलीकुचतटाहतिजातभयैरिव ।
अपसृतैरजनि प्रतिवासरं नृपतिगेहविहारसरोजलैः ।।२०।।

Day by day, waters in the pleasure-lakes in the palace-gardens of the king were found diminishing further and further from the shore. This made one fancy that they were getting more and more afraid of receiving knocks from the breasts of Kuntala damsels who delighted in sporting in them. (20)

प्रचुरघर्मपयःकणजालिकागुणितमौक्तिकमण्डनशालिभिः ।
नवशिरीषवतंसमनोहरैः सुवदना वदनैस्तममोदयन् ।।२१।।

The king was delighted with the bare faces of his beautiful ladies with the *śirīṣa* wreaths placed on the ear, and pearl-like drops of sweat appearing on their body and face. (21)

दिनविरामविकस्वरमल्लिकाकुसुमसौरभहारिषु सुभ्रुवाम् ।
कचभरेषु निवेशयतो मुखं नरपतेर्न वितृष्णमभून्मनः ।।२२।।

The king could not contain his emotion when his eyes fixed to the braids of hair on the heads of his charming women, which blew sweet fragrance emanating from the evening blossoms of *kuṭaja* flowers with which they were decked. (22)

हिमगृहेषु निरन्तरशीकरप्रकरदर्शिततारकपङक्तिषु ।
दिवसतापमहापयदायतं वरवधूसहितो वसुधाधिपः ।।२३।।

The king got over the heat of the day by retiring with the choicest ladies to his summer house where water particles, sparkling like stars, were being sprayed continuously. (23)

अथ दलन्निचुलद्रुममञ्जरीनिचयदर्शितचामरविभ्रमः ।
कृतनुतिः किल चातकयाचकैर्नृपतिमन्वगमज्जलदागमः ।।२४।।

After summer, winter arrived, *cātaka* birds welcomed it with joy, and which by the flowering of *nicula* reeds, produced the illusion of *cauri*s. (24)

तत इतो विहरत्तटिदङ्गनाललितलास्यहरिन्मणिमण्डपैः ।
पटुमृदङ्गरवोपमगर्जितैर्निबिडमाविरभूयत वारिदैः ।।२५।।

Thick clouds began to appear here and there. They looked like the sporting pavilions of women called lightening and the thunder that was heard resembled the sounds of *mr̥daṅga* drums. (25)

स्फुटतटित्तपनीयगुणोज्ज्वलैः पृथुपयःकणमौक्तिकसङ्गिभिः ।
अलिकदम्बकसच्छविभिर्दिशामसितकञ्चुलिकायितमम्बुदैः ।।२६।।

The black beetle like clouds looked like dark coloured petticoats, flashes of lightening that appeared now and then glittered like borders of gold-lace, and rain drops like pearl-counting's. (26)

हरितलोहितपाण्डुरराजत त्रिदशराजशरासनलेखिका ।
मरतकोपलविद्रुममौक्तिकैर्विरचिता रशनेव नभःश्रियः ।।२७।।

The rainbow with its colours, green, red, and white, Shone like the girdle, set with emerald, coral and pearl of the beautiful sky goddesses. (27)

रुधिरबिन्दुनिभच्छविरन्वगात् क्षितितले हरिगोपपरम्परा ।
घमघरट्टपरस्परघट्टनक्षरदिरम्भदवह्निकणावलिम् ।।२८।।

Red insects looking like blood drops, began to swarm the earth. They looked like the sparks of the lightening fire that had dropped down on earth when clouds collided with clouds in a violent manner. (28)

पटुपुरःपवनाविगतभ्रमा जलमुचः करकोपलकैतवात् ।
सलिलराशिपयस्सहचूषितामुदवमन्निव मौक्तिकसंहतिम् ।।२९।।

Hail stones fell from clouds that whirled round with the blowing of the eastern wind. Looking at them, one wondered if they were not pearls which were taken along with the sea-water during the latter's formation. (29)

अभिमते सति वारिधरोदये मधुरषड्जमनोहरगीतिभिः ।
गिरितटीषु मुहुः परिमण्डलीकृतकलापमनर्ति शिखण्डिभिः ।।३०।।

In mountainous plateau peacocks danced singing sweet notes of *ṣaḍja* at the emergence of clouds that were their favourites. (30)

पटुतटिद्द्रुणकोणहताः पुरो रतिपतेः पटहा इव दिव्यकाः ।
निशमिताः स्फुटसाहसमध्वगैर्जलधरा वियदध्वनि दध्वनुः ।।३१।।

Travellers with distressed courage heard the thundering of clouds in the sky which sounded like celestial kettledrums which cupid beat with sticks of lightning. (31)

दलितकन्दलमुच्छ्वसदर्जुनं स्फुटकदम्बमुदाञ्चितकैतकम् ।
मुदितचातकमुन्मुखबर्हिणं कतिचिदास दिनानि वनान्तरम् ।।३२।।

For some days the forest presented this appearance; plantains put forth new shoots. *Arjuna* trees blossomed and also the *kadamba* and *ketaka*. *Cātaka* birds were in great excitement, along with the peacocks. (32)

करतलैरिव गन्धवहैर्घनाः प्रहितकैतकपांसुविभूतयः ।
स्तनितहुंकृतिभिर्निरकासयन् नृपतियौवतमानमहाग्रहम् ।।३३।।

Through winds, as if with hands, clouds sprinkled *ketaka* dusts resembling holy ashes. The murmuring of thunder was like the humming and all this was effective in banishing the evil spirit of love-anger which sometimes possessed the ladies of the harem. (33)

चलितबर्हिणचन्द्रकचित्रितैः सुरभिगन्धिशिलामदशालिभिः ।
विकचनीपवनैर्नृपतेर्मनो मुहुरहारि विहारमहीधरैः ।।३४।।

The mind of the king was very much attracted by the pleasure hillocks. Even in the tails of dancing peacocks rendered them very charming, and camphor deposits in them exuded the most pleasing smell. The numberless *kadamba* trees there were in full blossom. (34)

तमहरन्नहरत्ययमालतीकुसुमदन्तुरकुन्तलकान्तयः ।
परिहितागरुधूपितवाससः सुतनवो मृगनाभिसुगन्धयः ।।३५।।

The king was also attracted by his beautiful ladies whose curling locks were decorated with the evening blossoms of *mālatī* flowers. Their clothes were scented with fumes of aloewood, and they sweet smelled like musk. (35)

मणिमयानि गृहाणि समीरणाः कुटजकैतकसौरभवाहिनः ।
मदकलाश्च गिरः प्रचलाकिनां क्षितिपतेः स्मरदीपकतां ययुः ।।३६।।

The king's passion of love was very much excited by gem-set pavilions of scented breezes, floating the smell of *kuṭaja* and *ketaka* flowers. And by the musical notes of inebriated peacocks. (36)

नववधूपरिरम्भणदोहलान्यनुपदं निनदैः प्रतिपादयन् ।
अलभत क्षणदासु घनागमो नरपतेः किल नर्मसुहृत्पदम् ।।३७।।

The arrival of the cloudy season performed the role of a romance intimate to the king in the night time, as it made even the newly-married shy girls hug him at each sound of thunder-murmurings. (37)

तदनु पद्मवनीपरिहासकस्त्रिदशनाथशरासनतस्करः ।
भुजगभुङ्मुखमुद्रणभौरिकः समुदभूत् समयो जलदात्ययः ।।३८।।

Then autumn arrived, lotus-clusters that made the jester to laugh, the thief that stole rainbow, like the treasury officer sets his seal, that shut the mouths of peacocks. (38)

विधुतकाशसटाभरभासुरः प्रकटितोरुजपारुणलोचनः ।
व्यघटयद् घनदन्तिघटाः स्फुरद्रविमुखः शरदागमकेसरी ।।३९।।

The season resembled a lion in dispersing the elephant-like clouds. His face was the sun. The *kāśa*s were his mane and the bloosming china roses, his red eyes. (39)

अवितथं रजनीदिवसाधिपौ मधुरिपोर्नयने इति भाषितम् ।
स्फुटममुष्य यतः स्वपनात्ययादजनि तादृशमुन्मिषितं तयोः ।।४०।।

It was no empty saying that the sun and the moon are the eyes of Viṣṇu. Now that he was woken up from sleep, thus they also opened in their proper splendour. (40)

कलशजस्य मुनेरुदयाज्जहुः कलुषतां सलिलानि महौजसः ।
सदुपदेशवशादिव शासितुस्तनुभृतां हृदयानि दयानिधेः ।।४१।।

By reason of the rise of the brilliant Agastya star, the waters were cleared of their muddy condition and shone as clear as the minds of men who had received proper instruction from a merciful *guru*. (41)

विशदशारदनीरदशारितं वियदलक्ष्यत वीततटिद्गुणम् ।
प्रकटफेनकदम्बककर्बुरं जलमिवाम्बुनिधेर्गतविद्रुमम् ।।४२।।

White clouds lined the sky, and lightning disappeared. In that state the sky resembled the watery expanse of the sea with clusters of foam here and there and coral reefs disappeared. (42)

नियतमम्बुदशाणनिघर्षणादतिमहस्कमहस्करमण्डलम् ।
अजनि वर्षविधोरपि वार्षिकैर्जलधरैः परिधौतमिवोज्ज्वलम् ।।४३।।

The clouds in winter seemed to have acted like a whetstone and a wash in the case of the sun and the moon, respectively, for they both shine now with increased brightness and splendour.(43)

जलदकालकलिस्फुरितां शनैः कलुषतां प्रशमय्य कृशाः पुनः ।
घटयति स्म शरत् तटिनीसखीरुपनतैः कलहंसविलासिभिः ।।४४।।

The rivers were rid of impurities and looked slimmer. And by uniting them with the swans, their lovers, the season really enacted the role of a dear female friend effecting reconciliation between angry lovers. (44)

सरसिजाकरसञ्चरदिन्दिराचरणहंसकनिक्कणमन्थरः ।
मदनमङ्गलतूर्यरवोऽभवन्मदकलः कलहंसकुलध्वनिः ।।४५।।

Everywhere heard the charming sounds of swans resembling jingles of the music of Lakṣmī's feet wandering on lotus beds or like the auspicious resonance of cupid's *tūrya* (musical instruments). (45)

विकचपद्मविलोचनमात्मनो मुखमवेक्षितुमात्तकुतूहला ।
नियतमभ्रनिचोलकगर्भतः शरदकर्षदहर्पतिदर्पणम् ।।४६।।

Autumn, like a beautiful lady with lotus eyes, desired as it were to see her face every now and then in the mirror of the sun whom she frequently drew out from his wrapper of white clouds. (46)

विलसदुत्पललोचनशालिनीः स्फुरितचन्द्रमुखीः कुमुदस्मिताः ।
नरपतिः स्फुटतारकहारिणीर्निरविशद् दयिता इव यामिनीः ।।४७।।

The king enjoyed the autumnal nights fully; for in their contents they resembled his ladies in every esteem; blue water lilies had the beauty of their eyes, the moon of their face. White water lilies, of their smile and stars of the pupil of their eyes. (47)

परिणतेक्षुपरिच्युतमौक्तिकग्रथितहारमनोहरमूर्तिभिः ।
विशदमस्य यशो नृपतेः कलं कलमगोपवधूभिरगीयत ॥४८॥

The young women guarding rice fields sang the spotless fame of the king, decked as their persons were with garlands of pearls that had come out of the bursting of ripe red sugar cane. (48)

दलदयुग्मदलोदरसौरभप्रसरपक्ष्मलिता वनवायवः ।
मुहुरधःकृतयन्तृनिवारणानकृषत क्षितिभृन्मदवारणान् ॥४९॥

Elephants in rut, again and again, pulled the chains with which they were fastened, as forest winds laden with the smell of blossoming *saptaparṇa* trees blew over their bodies. (49)

वनभुवः परितः पवनेरितैर्नवजपाकुसुमैः कृतदीपिकाः ।
प्रथममेव नृपस्य निदेशतो विजयिनस्तुरगान् निरराजयन् ॥५०॥

Everywhere forests were adorned with blossoming china roses, and as they stirred in the wind, it looked as if, by orders of the king, they were waving auspicious flame to his victorious horses before any others did so. (50)

अथ नृपस्य समुत्सुकचेतसो [मदन*]केलिकलासु विलासिनः ।
प्रियमिवा[चरितुं*]समुपागमत् प्रणदयन्(?) क्षणदास्तुहिनागमः ॥५१॥

Then making the nights long, as if to please the amours king who loved to enjoy night sports very much, there arrived the dewy season. (51)

हिमभरैर्विहतः कमलाकरो मृदितकान्तिरभून्मृगलाञ्छनः ।
वदनमेव नरेन्द्रनतभ्रुवामभजत श्रियमप्रतिशासनाम् ॥५२॥

Lotus clusters were hit by snow and the moon became pale in colour. Only the faces of the king's beloved consorts grown in unmatched charm. (52)

पुलककञ्चुकितैः कुचमण्डलैः स्फुरितसीत्कृतिभिश्च मुखेन्दुभिः ।
अविरतं स्मरतन्त्रमिवान्वभूदवनिपालविलासवतीजनः ॥५३॥

The royal ladies, as they shivered in cold, seemed to be in an endless state of passion of love. The hairs in their breasts always stood in horripilation and their mouths uttering murmuring sounds. (53)

विकचकुन्दकलापपरिष्क्रियाविरचितालकजालकविभ्रमम् ।
असमयेऽपि समौक्तिकमण्डनं प्रभुरमंस्त निजं प्रमदाजनम् ॥५४॥

The king's beloveds made him believe that they were decking their hair with pearls, in out of season, as the clusters of their curls were always dressed with the white blossoms of jasmine. (54)

बहलकुङ्कुमपङ्कविलेपनप्रसृमरोष्मपयोधरमण्डलैः ।
अरमताविरतं रमणीजनैरगरुगन्धिषु गर्भगृहेषु सः ॥५५॥

The king loved to remain in his inner apartments, amiably scented with *agāru* fumes, in friendship of his beautiful consorts whose breasts were warm and smeared with saffron paste. (55)

इति सुखान्युचितानि हिमागमे समनुभूय मनोभवसन्निभः ।
शिशिरयामवतीष्वपि रागवान् रमयितुं रमणीरुदयुङ्क्त सः ॥५६॥

The king like the incarnated cupid in his personal charm, thus enjoying the comforts of the cold season, desired to sport with his ladies in the nights in spite of the cold weather. (56)

शबलितान्यलिकागरुबिन्दुभिश्चलदृशां रतिविभ्रमसूचकैः ।
नवलवङ्गतरुप्रसवास्तृतान्यभजतानुनिशं शयितानि सः ॥५७॥

He very much liked to lie down on beds speckled with fresh foliage of clove plants, beds that were also dotted with particles of *agāru* fallen from the forehead of his ladies in their passionate performances. (57)

परिलसन्नवलोध्ररजोभरच्छुरणपाण्डरगण्डतलैर्मुखैः ।
मृगमदद्रवचारुविशेषकैर्मृगदृशो नृपतेरहरन् मनः ।।५८।।

His ladies presented a particularly attractive appearance to the king, with their faces white with the dust of *lodhra* flowers and with their foreheads anointed with musk paste. (58)

अपदिशञ्छिशिरानिलमङ्गकैः पुलकितैर्नृपतैः सविधं गतः ।
मदनसंभृतघर्मपयःकणैर्भृशमलज्जत मुग्धबधूजनः ।।५९।।

Young girls, who got horripilation by reason of their unmistakable love passion, began to gather. (59)

द्विगुणयन्नधरव्रणवेदनां कृतकचग्रहणैः परिचुम्बनैः ।
कपटरोषकषायितलोचनं निभृतहासमवैक्ष्यत यौवतैः ।।६०।।

Young ladies pretended anger, but glad at heart, looked at the king, as he practised acts of love, such as biting the lips, drawing by the hair, and kissing all over. (60)

विकलकञ्चुकलक्ष्यन(व?ख)व्रणं विगतमौक्तिकहारमनोहरम् ।
तरुणिमोष्मनखम्पचमङ्गनास्तनयुगं हिमहारि विभोरभूत् ।।६१।।

The breasts of his ladies warm with blossoming youthfulness drove away the cold of the season when the king casted longing looks on them; they were very beautiful in their semi-covered state with marks of nails, and without the strings of pearls on them. (61)

उपहरन् कुसुमानि महीरुहां किसलयैः कलिसाञ्जलिबन्धनः ।
मधुरकोकिलकूजितभाषितो मधुरथैनमुपपासितुमासदत् ।।६२।।

Then spring approached, with trees full of flowers as if for an offering with sprouting foliage-like hands folded in veneration. With the cooing of cuckoos, as if uttering humble words of obeisance, the season seemed to have come to pay homage to the king. (62)

मधुसुगन्धि रजः सहकारजं मलयशैलसमीरणमान्त्रिकाः ।
प्रणयरोषपराङ्मुखमानिनीहृदयसंवननार्थमिवाकिरन् ।।६३।।

The gentle southern breeze that blew scattering fragrant mango flowers dust seemed like magicians smattering ashes to turn the mind of anger-ridden damsels that disdained their lovers. (63)

उपवनेष्वगमन्नुपमेयतां स्फुटरुचो नवकिंशुककुट्मलाः ।
मथितपान्थमृगक्षतजारुणैर्मदनकेसरिणः कुटिलैर्नखैः ।।६४।।

Kiṁśuka trees with buds of amazing red shine like false nails of lovely travellers which resembled the blood-stained nails of lion that had torn the deer. (64)

चटुलषट्पदकज्जलपातिनी विरुरुचे नवचम्पकमञ्जरी ।
प्रकटितेव हिमापगमश्रिया स्मरमहोत्सवदीपपरम्परा ।।६५।।

Rows of clusters of *campaka* flowers with collyrium-like beetles settling on them looked like lamps lighted by the spring in celebration of cupid's festival. (65)

मधुनि मुग्धदृशां मुखसंस्तवात् तदनुषङ्गितया बकुलेषु च ।
मरुति चैतदनुक्षण[सौहृ*]दात् समुचितोऽजनि सौरभसङ्क्रमः ।।६६।।

The sweet aroma of wine in the mouths of beautiful-eyed ladies passed to the *bakula* flowers from which the southern breeze received it. Thus it had its dispersal in an suitable way. (66)

क्वणितनूपुरकुन्तलकामिनीचरणपङ्कजसङ्गवशादिव ।
मुखरभृङ्गमशोकमहीरुहैस्तदनुरूपमधार्यत पल्लवम् ।।६७।।

*Aśoka*s, with bees humming around in thick rows, indicated a sort of appropriateness to the manure which the tree had by the touch of the tender feet of Kuntala ladies resounding with ornaments. (67)

वरवधूपरिरम्भरसोल्लसल्ललितकुट्मलकण्टकिताकृतिः ।
कुरवकः कुसुमेषुमचेतनेष्वपि विश्रृङ्खलवृत्तिमसूचयत् ।।६८।।

The *kuruvaka*s that looked like hairs standing on end in the act of mutual embrace of lovers, raised passion even in the hearts of lifeless beings. (68)

पथिक [सार्थ*]पराक्रमणोत्सुकप्रसवकार्मुककाहलनिस्वनः ।
मधुरपञ्चमरागरसाञ्चितो जगदरञ्जयदन्यभृतध्वनिः ॥६९॥

The lovable *pañcama* notes of cuckoos delighted the world immensely. Lonely travellers that heard it felt as if they heard sounds of cupid's bow shooting arrows at them. (69)

अधिगताभिनवार्तवसम्पदः स्तबकसंजनितस्तनविभ्रमाः ।
भ्रमरकामुकसंवननक्षमा वनलता ललितां दधिरे दशाम् ॥७०॥

Wild creepers that were the beloved of the beetles attracted the latter very much as clusters of buds looking like breasts sprouted in them, in the flowering spring season. (70)

सुतनवः फलकेषु मधूत्सवे रतिपतिं परिलेखितुमुद्यताः ।
हृदयगोचरतामनिशं गतं **हरिहरा**त्मजमेव समालिखन् ॥७१॥

In the spring festival ladies wanted to paint forms of cupid on picture boards. But they ended by painting the form of King Kampana who was always in their heart. (71)

[म*]दनबेरनि(भां?भं)निभृतं पुरः क्षितिपतिं कृतचन्दनचर्चिकाः ।
अधिकघर्मपयोभिरवागमन् मृगदृशो विकसंत्पुलकैः करैः ॥७२॥

Certain ladies smeared the cupid-like person of the king with sandal paste, and their hands evidenced passion of love by sweat drops and horripilation that marked them in the act. (72)

मुखरकङ्कणमाकुलमेखलं चलितहाररलतं लुलितालकम् ।
अधिगतश्रममस्य वधूजनो रतिविशेषमशिक्षत डोलबा ॥७३॥

The tinkling of bracelets, the fling of gridles, the dropping of garlands and the flying of curls that marked the practice in swing play, looked like a rehearsal on the part of lovely ladies of love sports with their lover. (73)

उचितरागविशेषमनोहरे रतिपतेरुपगामविधौ स्त्रियः ।
नृपतिगोत्रकृतस्खलना ययुः प्रियसखीसविधेषु विलक्षताम् ॥७४॥

Some queens felt ashamed before their female companions

and in singing songs in praise of Kāma they often introduced the name of the king in their forgetfulness. (74)

क्षितिपतिं किल कुङ्कुममुष्टिना समभिताडयितुं धियमादधौ ।
सपदि धर्मपयःप्रसरेण तं विगलितं न विवेद वधूजनः ।।७५।।

They desired to splatter on the king paste of saffron, but they were not aware that the substance had already leaked out of their sweat suffused hands. (75)

इति समुपचिताभिश्चातुरीभिर्विशेषान्
ऋतुषु समुपलभ्यान् निर्विशन् निर्विशङ्कम् ।
सुतनुभिरवियोगोत्कण्ठिताभिस्तृतीयं
व्यतनुत पुरुषार्थं **कम्पराजः** कृतार्थम् ।।७६।।

King Kampana thus experienced the third end of life (Kāma) fruitful by sporting to his heart's content with the ladies of his harem whose passion was not dimmed even in busted union. (76)

।। इति [श्रीगङ्गादेव्या विरचिते मधुराविजयम्-
नाम्नि वीर*]कम्परायचरिते पञ्चमः सर्गः ।।

Thus ends the fifth canto, of the life of Vīra Kamparāya known as *Madhurāvijayam* composed by Śrī Gaṅgādevī.

षष्ठः सर्गः

Canto 6

अथ वरतनुभिः समं कदाचिद् विरचयितुं कसुमापचायलीलाम् ।
प्रमदवनममर्त्यकामिनीभिर्हरिरिव नन्दनमासदन्नरेन्द्रः ।।१।।

Like Hari (Lord Kr̥ṣṇa) always attended by celestial nymphs, the king with his ladies moved to his pleasure garden to gather flowers. Which reminded of the divine Nandana garden. (1)

मुखरितमणिमेखलाकलापाः प्रचलितमन्वचलंस्तमायताक्ष्यः ।
उपवनलतिका इवोपगीतभ्रमरकुला मलयाद्रिगन्धवाहम् ।।२।।

Royal women followed the king as hc started to move to the garden, with their tinkling jewelled girdles. That sight was like a line of humming beetles moving in the swirl of the fragrant southern Malaya wind. (2)

परिवहदनुरागपूरकल्पैः पदगलितैरथ यावकैर्वधूनाम् ।
सरणिररुणतामतीव नीता समजनि नूतनपल्लवास्तृतेव ।।३।।

The walking way of the royal women was smeared by the red lac-dye dripping from their feet, and it seemed as if a cover of tender leaves was being placed on the floor. (3)

विविधविलसितैर्विलासिनीनामसितसितारुणकान्तिभिः कटाक्षैः ।
कुवलयकुमुदारविन्दमालाखचितमिवामलमम्बरं बभासे ।।४।।

Shining side glances of ladies with blue, white and red tinge resembled the sky speckled with blue,white lotuses along with bloomed red lotuses. (4)

अजनयदवनीश्वरस्य चेतस्यसितदृशां मणिनूपुरप्रणादः ।
सहपरिचलितप्रसूनकेतोरवनमदैक्षवचापघोषशङ्काम् ।।५।।

The resonance of jewelled anklets of ladies, as it reached the king's ears produced the inkling in his mind, that it might be the blare of the stringing of cupid's bow. (5)

अवनिपतिमनुप्रतस्थुषीणां हरिणदृशामितरेतरप्रसक्ताः ।
मधुरसमधुरा गिरस्तदानीं बहुविधभङ्गितरङ्गिता बभूवुः ॥६॥

Ladies immersed in common conversations followed the king like flock of deers, as they followed the king, their various types of walk with the (jingling anklets) were like hearing the music in various notes. (6)

वरतनु ! परतः प्रयाहि मन्दं हरिणदृशां पुरतः प्रयायिनीनाम् ।
पथि गतिरयशीर्णहारमुक्तामणिगणशर्करिले पदं न कुर्याः ॥७॥

Oh you the beautiful friend! go slowly after the rest, otherwise you may injure your feet by trampling on the pearls dropped down on the way from the broken necklaces. (7)

नलिनमुखि ! न बोधय प्रसुप्तानिह मणिनूपुरशिञ्जितेन हंसान् ।
द्रुतगमनविघातमाचरेयुर्नियतममी तव पादपद्मलग्नाः ॥८॥

Oh lotus faced! with the tinkles of your jewelled anklets sleeping swans will wake up and will surround your feet by mistake thinking your feet for lotuses and thus cause hindrance to your quick movement. (8)

करनखरमरीचिमञ्जरीभिर्हृतहृदयो जलशङ्कया कुरङ्गः ।
अनुपतति विलोकयैकवारं सखि! नियतं स निवर्तते विलक्षः ॥९॥

Look you here friend, this thirsty deer, which eagerly approaching you mistaking the brightness radiating from your fingernails for water, will surely move away in ignominy, once the mistake is found. (9)

शशिमुखि! शशिकान्तकुट्टिमेषु स्खलनमिया न पदात् पदं प्रयासि ।
इयमिह वदनानुबिम्बराजिस्तव न पुनर्नवपङ्कजोपहारः ॥१०॥

The moon-faced dear, do not move ahead; if you move a step ahead, you may hit against the moonstone wall. But the manifestation of your lotus-like face has already penetrated into it. (10)

किमिति मृदुपदं प्रयासि मुग्धे! ननु कितवः सह याति कामिनीभिः ।
नवकुसुमरजोन्धकारबन्धैरभिसरणार्हमिदं वनं दिवापि ।।११।।

Oh, my foolish, friend! why do you walk so slowly? You do not seem to realize that your mischievous lover will exploit this to court the company of other women. In this darkish pleasure forest, with thick dust of fresh flowers is eminently fitted for secret meeting even in the day time. (11)

अथ विदितमियं द्रुता गतिस्ते मुखभवलोकयितुं निवृत्य भर्तुः ।
न किमलमपराङ्गमेव तावद् दयिततमस्य मृगीदृशां मनांसि ।।१२।।

Oh friend! I know you walk very fast so that you may surpass your lover in order to look back and see his face. But you do not seem to realize that women in their minds have the lovers face always in front of them. (12)

स्तनजघनभरं तवालि! जाने तदपि गतिस्त्वरया त्वया विधेया ।
न कलयसि निरन्तरं निषेव्या युवतिजनैर्बहु* .... ।।१३।।

I know you could not walk fast because of your heavy breasts. But, friend, you must walk fast. (13)

***Ślokas* 14 to 56 are damaged and not accessible in the manuscripts**

....पतन्ति ।
मदनसुभटवारणास्त्रशङ्कां मनसि चकार चकोरलोचनानाम् ।।५५।।

करयुगकलितप्लवः प्रियाणां परिचलितोरुनितम्बमण्डलानाम् ।
..........नच्छलादकार्षीत् सुरतगुरुः पुरुषायितोपदेशम् ।।५६।।

अवनिपतिरसि(श्च?क्त) दीर्घिकाया मुखकमलं सलिलेन साभिलाषम् ।
किमपि समधिकार्द्रपक्ष्मलेखं वदनमभूदरुणेक्षणं परस्याः ।।५७।।

In the pleasure lake the king splashed water on a lotus and this made a lady besides him cast on him angry looks of jealousy,

* तालपत्रादर्शे इत ऊर्ध्वे ४१ श्लोका न दृश्यन्ते ।

along with the tears in the fringes of her eyes, so eyelashes were wet. (57)

प्रणयिनि सलिलापवारितेन स्पृशति करेण सलीलमूरुमूलम् ।
प्रकटितशफराभिघातभी(तं?ति) र्मिषति जनेऽप्यमुमालिलिङ्ग
काचित् ।।५८।।

The king, underneath the water, touched the upper part of a lady's thigh, she pretended it as if a fish-bite and hugged her lover even when her companions were looking on. (58)

सलिलहतिभियापवृत्तगात्र्याः प्रचलितवेण्यपराङ्गकं परस्याः ।
धरणिपतिरमस्त मीनकेतोः फलकमुपाहितखड्गवल्लरीकम् ।।५९।।

Another lady, afraid of being struck with splashes of water, abruptly turned, her braid of hair falling in front. The king cast longing glances on it, as if it were cupid's part with his sword placed on it. (59)

चरणविलुठितो विलङ्घितोरुः परिगतनीविरवाप्तनाभिचक्रः ।
स्तनतटलुलितः क्रमेण तासां मुखशशिबिम्बमचुम्बदम्बुपूरः ।।६०।।

The mass of water first touched the feet, then the thighs, then the cloth, then the waist and then the breasts of beautiful ladies as they slowly slide down it. (60)

विशदनखपदं वपुः सपत्न्या....नव पश्यति निर्निमेषमस्मिन् ।
व्यधित विहृतिकैतवेन काचित् प्रहितजला परिमीलिताक्षमेनम् ।।६१।।

A lady blinded the king by splashing water, as if in sport, against his eyes when the other ladies turned to look at the nail marks on the body of her rival. (61)

विशदमधरमक्ष्यनञ्जनाभं विगतललाम वितन्वती ललाटम् ।
रतिरिव जलकेलिरङ्गनानामवनिपतेः स्पृहणीयतामयासीत् ।।६२।।

Sporting in the waters made the ladies looked as if they had just had their sexual pleasure. Their lips were colour-free, their eyes devoid of collyrium and their foreheads without the red mark. And with such a sight the king greatly pleased. (62)

परिमुषितपटीरलेपनेप्व[प्य*]विरललग्नसरोजकेसरेषु ।
कुचकलशतटेषु **कुन्तलीनां** नखरपदानि न लक्षितान्यभूवन् ॥६३॥

From the breasts of Kuntala ladies sandal paste was washed away, and the cover of lotus dust which took its place efficiently masked all nail marks on them. (63)

विहृतिरयपरिच्युतान् बतंसानसितदृशामनुदद् बहिः प्रवाहः ।
नहि जडिमसमन्वितोऽपि कोऽपि श्रुतिविषयात् पतितैः करोति मैत्रीम् ॥६४॥

The current of water floated away the flowers that had dropped from the ears (*śruti*) of ladies. Who will make friendship with persons not abiding the path of Śruti's (Vedas)? (64)

अपि दयिततमेन वारिताभिर्गृहसरसो विजहे न वारि ताभिः ।
परिलुलितललामचर्चिकाभिर्विहृतिरसान्महिलामचर्चिकाभिः ॥६५॥

Though their royal lover asked them to stop, the ladies had no mind to do so, as they were very much involved by the love of sport, and so they did not leave the pleasure lake though its water had completely washed away their decorative marks. (65)

अथ विहरणखेदमन्थराभिः सह निरगात् सरसो नृपः प्रियाभिः ।
कलशजलनिधेरिवाप्सरोभिर्बिबुधतरुर्मथनश्रमालसाभिः ॥६६॥

Then, at last tired of sports, they came out; the king started to (home) with them; he then resembled the *kalpavṛkṣa* moving from the milky ocean in the company of water nymphs exhausted with the tossings in churning. (66)

स्फुटनखरदनाङ्कमङ्गनानां परिलगदार्द्रदुकूलदर्शितोरु ।
वपुरनुकलमैक्षत क्षितीशो जलकणदन्तुरदीर्घकुन्तलाग्रम् ॥६७॥

The king was pleased to look at his beloved ones as they emerged out of the lake, with distinctly visible nail marks on their body, with their thighs revealed through the waving cover of wet clothing, and water particles dripping from their long braids of hair. (67)

चिकुरनियमनेषु कामिनीनामभिनववस्त्रपरिग्रहान्तरेषु ।
अभिमतपददर्शनैरयत्नैरतिमदनं स्वममंस्त **कम्पराजः** ।।६८।।

King Kampana thought himself more fortunate than even cupid, as he feasted his eyes on the body of his ladies between tying their hair and wearing fresh dress. (68)

ततः सैरन्ध्रीभिः कृतसमुचिताकल्परचनः
पुरन्ध्रीभिः सार्धं समधिगतशुद्धान्तवसतिः ।
त्रयीगीतं तेजस्त्रिपुरहरमाराध्य विधिवद्
यथार्हैर्व्यापारैर्नरपतिरहश्शेषमनयत् ।।६९।।

Then, dressing maids put his royal garments on him, and he left for his harem, and after offering due worship to Śiva, whose glory is sung by the Vedas, attended to duties of state for the rest of the day. (69)

।। इति [श्रीगङ्गादेव्या विरचिते मधुराविजयम्-
नाम्नि वीर*]कम्परायचरिते षष्ठः सर्गः ।।

Thus ends the sixth canto, of the life of Vīra Kamparāya known as *Madhurāvijayam* composed by Śrī Gaṅgādevī.

सप्तमः सर्गः

Canto 7

अथ **कम्पन**नरेन्द्रसुभ्रुवां मुखपद्मान्यनुहार्य पङ्कजैः ।
अपराधभियेव भानुमानपरक्ष्माधरकन्दरामगात् ।।१।।

Then the sun as if frightened of the fault he had given to the queens by making lotuses emulate the beauty of their faces sunk into the caverns of western mountains. (1)

परिचूषितदीप्तिरम्बुजैः पुनरूष्माणमिवाप्तुमौर्वतः ।
रयवल्गितवाहनो रविः पयसां राशिमवाप पश्चिमम् ।।२।।

From there he submerged into the waters of western ocean as if to replenish his heat from the underwater heat, the heat which had been spent in the day in making lotuses blossom. (2)

अपसर्पणसंभ्रमच्युतं दिनलक्ष्म्यास्तपनीयकुण्डलम् ।
रविमण्डलमाशशङ्किरे वरुणान्तःपुरवामलोचनाः ।।३।।

The ladies of Varuṇa's harem fancied the ball of the sun to be the golden earring which the goddesses of day had dropped down in their haste to leave. (3)

तरणेररुणीकृताः करैर्वरुणस्त्रैणकपोलभित्तयः ।
मदलोहिनिकामुपावहन् मदिरास्वादनमन्तराप्यहो ।।४।।

The cheeks of Varuṇa's ladies reddened with the rays of submerging sun and this change of colour came to their cheeks even when no intoxicating wine had been consumed. (4)

कमलोदरसंभृतं करैर्मधु पीत्वा रविरुज्झिताम्बरः ।
स्पृशति स्म दिशं प्रचेतसो न मदः कस्य विकारकारणम् ।।५।।

The sun getting drunk with the honey in the lotuses abandoned the sky and in that state touched the western region revered as Varuṇa's queen who is resistant to the harmful influence of drinking. (5)

प्रथमां हरितं प्रभाकरो विरहय्यात्मनि तापमाप यम् ।
अपरामुपगम्य तं जहौ हृदयं कः खलु वेत्ति रागिणाम् ।।६।।

The sun at one stage seemed to be badly affected with the heat of separation from eastern quarter but now he was seen enjoying himself in the company of the opposite quarter (western), his heat has gone on reaching her. The minds of lovers are undoubtedly enigmatic! (6)

परलोकपथं प्रपेदुषः पुनरावृत्तिमपेक्ष्य भास्वतः ।
मुकुलीभवदम्बुजच्छलादकरोदञ्जलिबन्धमब्जिनी ।।७।।

The lotus ponds with closed flowers looked as if offering their prayer with folded hands for the return of the sun who had left them for another hemisphere. (7)

प्रतिबिम्बपरम्पराम्बुधौ पवनोद्भूततरङ्गसङ्गिनी ।
नभसोऽवतरिष्यतो रवेर्मणिसोपानधियं व्यभावयत् ।।८।।

The ocean with the folds of evening clouds mirrored in the waves raised by wind looked as if setting up steps of gems for the sun to move down from the sky. (8)

चरमाम्बुधिवीचिचुम्बितप्रतिबिम्बाश्रयि मण्डलं रवेः ।
दिवसान्तनटस्य धूर्जटेर्विदधे काञ्चनतालविभ्रमम् ।।९।।

The globe of the setting sun as it touched its own reflection in the waves of western ocean elevated in one's mind the idea of golden cymbals for the evening dancer Śiva. (9)

चलचञ्चुपतद्बिसाङ्कुरैर्दिननाथार्पितदीनदृष्टिभिः ।
रजनीविरहव्यथातुरैरथ चक्राह्वयुगैरभूयत ।।१०।।

Cakravāka couple with their disgraceful looks at the setting sun and with fragments of lotus stalk falling from their beaks looked very miserable on the eve of their mutual separation of nightfall. (10)

उदधौ पतितस्य भास्वतः कतिभिश्चित् किरणैः खवर्तिभिः ।
उदपाद्यत कालकुञ्जरोद्दलिताहर्द्रुमशाखिकाभ्रमः ।।११।।

A few streaks of light still lined the sky even after the sun had sunk in the ocean waters. These streaks of light resembled the remnants of the branches of the tree of the day of which the time known as elephant was rooted out. (11)

पतयालुपतङ्गमण्डलक्षरदंशूत्कररञ्जिताकृतिः ।
मधुकैटभरक्तलोहितामुदधिः प्राप पुरातनीं दशाम् ॥१२॥

The ocean with the rays of setting sun reminded one of the time-honoured anecdote of its stained blood of Madhu and Kaiṭabha. (12)

गतदीप्ति गभस्तिमालिनो विलुठ[द् वीचिषु बिम्ब*]मम्बुधेः ।
शफराः फलखण्डशङ्कया रसनाभिर्लिलिहुर्मुहुर्मुहुः ॥१३॥

The sphere of the sun, losing its lustre rolled and scattered in the ocean waves. Sea fishes licked it again and again mistaking it for the broken remains of the fruit. (13)

स्खलितातपलेशमायतैर्विटपिच्छायशतैर्वृतं जगत् ।
भयविद्रवदर्कसैनिकं तिमिरैः क्रान्तमिवैक्ष्यत क्षणम् ॥१४॥

Small remnants of light caused hundreds of dark shadows of trees to be cast on the land. These resembled the army of darkness overwhelming the army of the fleeing sun in fear. (14)

प्रवसन् दिवसात्यये न्यधादुभयेषूभयमुष्णदीधितिः ।
हृदयेषु वियोगियोषितां परितापं त्विषमोषधीषु च ॥१५॥

The sun setting out on a journey at the end of the day entrusted his distress in heat, kept in the hearts of women separated from their lovers, was protected by the brilliance of plants which glowed in the night. (15)

खगमेकप्रवेक्ष्य तादृशं पतितं विष्णुपदातिलङ्घनात् ।
निभृतं चकिता इवाखिलास्तरुनीडेषु विलिल्यिरे खगाः ॥१६॥

Taking a warning as it were from the fall of the sun because of stepping on the feet of Viṣṇu, the birds quietly hid themselves in their nests in the trees. (16)

घटमानदलाररीपुटं नलिनं मन्दिरमिन्दिरास्पदम् ।
परिपालयति स्म निक्वणन् परितो यामिकवन्मधुव्रतः ।।१७।।

Within the closed petals of lotuses which are considered as Lakṣmī's dwelling houses the humming beetles moving around in swarms reminded of the night watchmen. (17)

अधिपङ्कजकोशमादधे बहिरालीनमधुव्रतच्छलात् ।
मधुसौरभरक्षणोत्सुका दिनलक्ष्मीरिव लक्ष्म जातुषम् ।।१८।।

The goddesses of the day sealed as it were the closed lotuses with the lack of beetles sitting close to their surface with a view to guard the fragrant treasure of honey within it. (18)

दिनवेषमपास्य यामिनीवपुषा कालनटस्य नृत्यतः ।
ददृशे जगता पितृप्रसूर्दिवि नेपथ्यपटीव पाटला ।।१९।।

The evening twilight was fancied by people as the screen of the stage where the dancer in time has to dance in the night having taken it as the mask of the day. (19)

रविरथ्यखुरोत्थितापरक्षितिभृद्गैरिकरेणुशोणया ।
क्षणमेकमकारि सन्ध्यया वरुणाशारुणकञ्चुकभ्रमः ।।२०।।

The same twilight raised the momentary vision of red jacket worn by the region of Varuṇa which got the characteristic fanciful colour by coming into contact with the dust raised by the hoofs of the sun's horses tramped on the red layers of the western mountain. (20)

वियति व्यरुचन् पयोधराः स्फुटसन्ध्यापरिपाटलत्विषः ।
अचिरावतरद्विभावरीपदलाक्षापटलानुकारिणः ।।२१।।

Travelling red clouds in the evening sky, resembling the cheeks of the maidens at night which just set foot on the horizon. (21)

नवपल्लवकोमलच्छविर्दिवि सान्ध्यो ददृशे महोभरः ।
(विनि?रवि)पातरयात् समुत्थितश्चरमाब्धेरिव विद्रुमोत्करः ।।२२।।

The reddish twilight-like tender leaves began to appear in the western horizon in the form of coral reefs given out by the western ocean in the disturbance caused by the rapid descend of the sun into its depth. (22)

उदियाय ततो दिगङ्गनाश्रवणाकल्पतमालपल्लवः ।
रजनीमुखपत्रलेखिकारचनारङ्कुमदस्तमोङ्कुरः ॥२३॥

Then darkness began to set in obscuring trees, sky and the area, giving rise to various fancies. (23)

किमु धूमभरः प्रशाम्यतो द्युमणिग्रावगतस्य तेजसः ।
प्रससार दिशस्तमोमिषात् किमु मीलत्कमलालिसञ्चयः ॥२४॥

There were tender leaves of *tamāla* which looked like the decoration of ears to the directions, and there the smeared musk paste looked like the drawings in the face of the night damsel. (24)

हलिहेतिदलत्कलिन्दजालहरीकन्दलकालिमद्रुहः ।
परितस्तरुरम्बरस्थलीं परितः स्थूलतमास्तमोभराः ॥२५॥

There was smoke rising from the cooling down of the sun's rays on earth surface; there beetles disguised as night darkness filling that region after leaving the closed lotuses; the black waters of the rivers were rising as tall as trees resembling the disturbances of the Yamunā River created by Śrī Kṛṣṇa at the time of Kālīya-mardana. (25)

नयनानि जनस्य तत्क्षणान्निरुणद्धि स्म निरन्तरं तमः ।
रविदीपभृताभ्रकर्परच्युतकालाञ्जनपुञ्जमेचकम् ॥२६॥

People felt as if they lost sight suddenly. It looked the power of the burning lamp of sun put off from the sky and from the lamp pot the lampblack was being scattered all around. (26)

तदमंसत मांसलं तमस्तनुतारागणबिन्दुजालकम् ।
दिवसात्ययचण्डताण्डवच्युतमीशस्य गजाजिनं जनाः ॥२७॥

The stars began to appear in the dark sky; it looked as if after the *tāṇḍava* dance of Śiva his clothing of elephant skin dotted with drops of blood. (27)

तिमि.............रोपमैस्तरलाभैरुदभावि तारकैः ।
परुषातपतापितात्मनो गगनस्येव निदाघबिन्दुभिः ॥२८॥

The stars looked as if they were drops of perspiration appearing on the blue sky as a result of the tormented burning heat of the sun during the day. (28)

अवपत् किमु कालकर्षकस्तिमिराम्भःकलुषे नभस्तले ।
विमलामुडुबीजमण्डलीं नवचन्द्रातपसस्यसिद्धये ॥२९॥

Time is like the ploughman, the stars were like well-washed seeds of grain, the dark skies were the muddy fields where the seeds were sown by him in order to raise the crop of moonlight; such was the fancy in the mind of people. (29)

अहरत्ययरागपल्लवस्तमसा कन्दलितो नभस्तरुः ।
सृजति स्म निरन्तरं हरिद्विटपैस्तारककोरकावलिम् ॥३०॥

The horizon resembled the fanciful tree. Twilight was the tender shoot, the darkness was the full-grown leaf, the regions were its branches and little stars were like its branches. (30)

अगमन्नभिसारिकाः प्रियाननुरागाञ्जनरञ्जितेक्षणाः ।
अभिनत्तिमिरेऽपि ताः पुनः श्वसितेनैव सुगन्धिना जनः ॥३१॥

Young women left to meet their lovers. But friends forbade them by their sighs that were made aware of them by the fragrance of their breath in the darkness. (31)

जननीमुपलभ्य यामिनीमधिकस्नेहदशाभिवर्धिताः ।
दिवसस्य लयं प्रपेदुषो गृहदीपा मुहुरर्भका इव ॥३२॥

Lamps lit in the houses which were like the children of mothers, night were tended with great care which took the form of oil wicks. (32)

उडुपुष्पकरम्बितं तमःकचभारं दधती निशीथिनी ।
अचिरादियमन्वपालयत् कुमुदस्मेरमुखी निशाकरम् ॥३३॥

The lady called darkness decorating her plait of hair with flowers of stars smilingly waited for a short time for her lover the moonlike the bloosoms of the white lilly. (33)

तदलु क्षणदागमोल्लसत्कलशाम्भोनिधिवीचिरोचिषः ।
व्यरुचन् कतिचित् कराङ्कुराः शशिनः शातमखे दिशामुखे ।।३४।।

Then a few rays of the moonlike glittering ocean waves were to be noticed in the eastern horizon. (34)

तरलालसतारकं मुखं कलयन्ती शरकाण्डपाण्डरम् ।
विगलत्तिमिराम्बरा बभौ हरिदैन्द्री हरिणाङ्कगर्भिणी ।।३५।।

The eastern quarter hiding the moon about to rise with her pale appearance looked like a woman's large abdomen with child whom she was about to be delivered. (35)

अथ किञ्चिददृश्यतैन्दवं वपुरार्द्रोदयरागलोहितम् ।
बलशासनदिग्विलासिनीमुखसिन्दूरललामकोमलम् ।।३६।।

A portion of the reddish sphere of the moon appeared on the eastern region like the mark on the forehead of a beautiful maiden whom that region might be imagined to incarnate. (36)

परिपिण्डितयावकारुणं प्रचकाशे हिमरश्मिमण्डलम् ।
रचितं नवरक्तसन्ध्यकैर्विजयच्छत्रमिवात्मजन्मनः ।।३७।।

The reddish sphere of the rising moon looked like the victorious umbrella of cupid made of red *sandhyaka* flowers. (37)

परुषेऽपि तथा प्रभानिधौ विधुरं लोकमिने परेयुषि ।
उदशिश्वसदादृतैःकरैरथ राजा मृदुभिर्नवोदयः ।।३८।।

Just as a new king who after the departure of the powerful personality of an old king ministers comfort the humanity by mild taxes so also the moon. After the splendorous sun had disappeared pleased the world with his cool pleasant rays. (38)

अथ **कम्पनृपो**ऽपि कृत्यवित् कृतसन्ध्यासमयोचितक्रियः ।
अवदत् सविधे स्थितां **प्रियां** भुवि **गङ्गेत्य**भिनन्दिताह्वयाम् ।।३९।।

Then the devoted king Kampana duly performed the worship of *sandhyā* and afterwards addressed his queen who was near and whom the world was overjoyed to call her as Gaṅgā. (39)

कमलाक्षि! कटाक्ष्यतामयं समयो वर्णनया रसार्द्रया ।
जन एष वचस्तवामृतं श्रवसा पाययितुं कुतूहली ।।४०।।

Oh my lotus-eyed dear! let this hour be honoured by your sweet description. This servant of yours eagerly waits to drink the nectar of your expression with his open ears. (40)

इति सा **दयितेन** भाषिता दरनम्रं दधती मुखाम्बुजम् ।
वदति स्म शनैः शुचिस्मिता सरसोदारपदां सरस्वतीम् ।।४१।।

Thus king spoken to her, the queen slightly lowered her lotus-like face in shy and slowly began to give utterance to her charming words. (41)

स्वदमानसुगन्धिमारुतः प्रसरत्कोमलचन्द्रिकोदयः ।
नृपचन्द्र! निरीक्ष्यतामयं [समयः*] पोषितपुष्पसायकः ।।४२।।

Oh my dearest! see how pleasant is the hour and how propitious is the cupid with the gently fragrant breeze and the just rising charming moon. (42)

परिरभ्य दृढं चिरागतः प्रथमाशासुदृशा निशापतिः ।
[श्लथयत्यय*]मंशुभिर्नखैस्तिमिरश्रेणिमयीं प्रवेणिकाम् ।।४३।।

The lord of night embrace the eastern region to his bosom passionately and with the nail like rays unties her braid of hair with which darkness is born. (43)

प्रथमाचलमौलिमुच्चकैरधिरुह्याम्बरपात्रसम्भृतम् ।
अयमंशुमृणालिकामुखैस्तिमिरं चूषयतीव चन्द्रमाः ।।४४।।

Having born from the eastern mountain the moon looks like sucking the darkness from the cup of sky his rays acting as lotus stalks to imbibe through it. (44)

अलिमीलमयस्तमोमयं प्रविलाप्योदयरागवह्निना ।
कलयत्ययमोषधीश्वरः कलधौतं शुचि कौमुदीमिषात् ।।४५।।

The moon who is the king of miraculous herbs practises alchemy as it were by transforming the iron called darkness into the silver called moonlight by subjecting it to flames by the process, called raising song – *udaya rāga* (sun rise or dawn). (45)

शशिमण्डलशङ्खपेटकादवकृष्य क्षपया समर्पितम् ।
कुमुदच्छवि कौमुदीमयं दधती क्षौममभाद् दिगङ्गना ।।४६।।

The young woman who called the eastern region to draw out her white silk of moonlight presented to her by night from the conch-white box of sphere of moon and adores herself with it, looked marvellous. (46)

हरितं परिरभ्य वासवीं हरिणाङ्कः करपातलीलया ।
स्पृशति प्रणयात् कुमुद्वतीं बत! विश्वासपदं न कामिनः ।।४७।।

The moon embraces with his hands of rays the damsel of eastern region and at the same time also touches another young lady called Kumudavatī – bed of night lotuses. This reminds one that the lustful men must not be trusted. (47)

मुहुरामृशदेव पद्मिनीमपि रागी क्षणदाकरः करैः ।
यदमुं प्रति नेयमुन्मुखी प्रभवत्यत्र पतिव्रतागुणः ।।४८।।

Though the moon touches incessantly with his rays as with hands, the clusters of lotuses do not turn back and look at him. This is a proof that virtuous women are firm in their vow of chastity. (48)

अनुदर्शमनुप्रवेशतस्तपनाच्छक्तिमवाप तापिनीम् ।
नियतं हिमदीधितिर्यतः क्षमते तापयितुं वियोगिनः ।।४९।।

The sun enters the moon at every new moon and so the latter is also endowed with the heating eminence of the former. This exhibits the case of lovers in separation. (49)

अलिविभ्रममन्तरेति यन्न विधोस्तन्मृगलक्ष्म किन्त्वयम् ।
पुरजिद्रथचक्रतार्जितो बहलः कज्जललेपकालिमा ।।५०।।

The black spot, observed on the moon like a black beetle in the centre of the moon's sphere, as some predict is not the sign of the dcer. But what it evidences is the lampblack which he had while being used as one of the wheels of Rudra's chariot at the time of destruction of Tripura. (50)

मघवन्मणिभङ्गमेचकः शशिनि श्यामलिमा चकास्ति यः ।
जनयत्ययमङ्कपालिकाप्रणयालीननिशीथिनीधियम् ।।५१।।
कलयामि कलङ्ककैतवान्नियतं धारयते.......... ।*

Otherwise you may consider that spot blue as *indranīla* gem as night herself who is his (moon's) darling lying there in love's repose. (51)

।। [इति श्रीगङ्गादेव्या विरचिते मधुराविजयम्-
नाम्नि वीरकम्परायचरिते सप्तमः सर्गः ।*] ।।

Thus ends the seventh canto of the life of Vīra Kamparāya known as *Madhurāvijayam* composed by Śrī Gaṅgādevī.

---

* इतः परमुपत्रिंशपद्यनिवेशपर्याप्तं पत्रं तालपत्रादर्शे न लिखितम् । "व्याघ्रपुरी" त्वादीनां वृत्तभेददर्शनादष्टमसर्गान्तर्भावः संभाव्यते ।

अष्टमः सर्गः

Canto 8

.... ।
..........................**व्याघ्रपुरी**ति सा यथार्थम् ॥१॥

........this means it is like Vyāghrapurī. (*Śloka* damaged and thus incomplete.) (1)

अधिरङ्गमवाप्तयोगनिद्रं हरिमुद्वेजयतीति जातभीतिः ।
पतितं मुहुरिष्टकानिकायं फणचक्रेण निवारयत्यहीन्द्रः ॥२॥

In Śrīraṅgam the lord of serpents is seen warding off the tumbling debris of bricks with his hood in case they fall and disturb the sleep of *yoga* in which Hari is enfolded there. (2)

.... ।
.....................................**गजप्रमाथिनाथः** ॥३॥

Śloka meaning is not clear to me except the last word which means "Head or lord of the elephants". (3)

घुणजग्धकवाटसम्पुटानि स्फुटदूर्वाङ्कुरसन्धिमण्डपानि ।
श्लथगर्भगृहाणि वीक्ष्य दूये भृशमन्यान्यपि देवताकुलानि ॥४॥

When I looked at the state of the temples of other gods, my distress knows no bounds. The breakdowns of their door are eaten up by termites. The arches over their inner shelters are let out with wild growth of vegetation. (4)

मुखराणि पुरा मृदङ्गघोषैरभितो देवकुलानि यान्यभूवन् ।
तुमुलानि भवन्ति फेरवाणां निनदैस्तानि भयङ्करैरिदानीम् ॥५॥

Those temples which were once resonant with the melody of *mṛdaṅga* drums are now echoing the fearful howls of jackals. (5)

अतिलङ्घ्य चिरन्तनीं स्वसीमामपदेष्वर्पितजीवनप्रवृत्तिः ।
मुहुरुत्पथगामिनी **तुलुष्का**नधुना हानुकरोति **सह्यकन्या** ॥६॥

Even Sahya *kanyā* has diverted her path flowing towards east, by seeing this one can gauze the atrocities of merciless tuluṣkās, even River Kaveri has lost her patience. (6)

सततार्ध्वरधूमसौरभैः प्राङ्निगमोद्घोषणवद्भिरग्रहारैः ।
अधुनाजनि विस्रमांसगन्धैरधिकक्षीब**तुलुष्क**सिंहनादैः ।।७।।

The brāhmaṇa streets, where once the sacrificial smoke was ever seen rising, and the chanting of Vedas always greeted the ears, now filled with the musty odour of meat, and resounds of the roars of lion-like drunken Turuṣkas. (7)

मधुरोपवनं निरीक्ष्य दूये बहुशः खण्डितनालिकेरषण्डम् ।
परितो नृकरोटिकोटिहारप्रचलच्छूलपरम्परापरीतम् ।।८।।

Very much I lament for what has happened to the gardens in Madhurā. The coconut trees have all been cut and in their place are to be seen rows of iron spikes with human skulls dangling at the points. (8)

रमणीयतरो बभूव यस्मिन् रमणीनां मणिनू पुरप्रणादः ।
द्विजशृङ्खलिकाखलात्कियाभिः कुरुते राजपथः स्वकर्णशूलम् ।।९।।

In the highways which were once charming with the sounds of anklets of beautiful women, are now heard ear-piercing noise of brāhmaṇas being dragged bound in iron fetters. (9)

परितस्तततन्तुवायतन्तुव्यतिषङ्गाज्जनितानि जालकानि ।
पुरगोपुरसालभञ्जिकानां दधते **चीन**पटावगुण्ठनत्वम् ।।१०।।

Webs formed by spiders have since taken the place of silk veils with which the dolls adorning the outer towers of the city were once covered. (10)

हिमचन्दनवारिसेकशीतान्यभवन् यानि गृहाङ्गणानि राज्ञाम् ।
हृदयं मम खेदयन्ति तानि द्विजबन्दीनयनाम्बुदूषितानि ।।११।।

Royal courtyards which were once cool with the spraying of ice-cold sandal water, now distress me, wet as they are with the tears of brāhmaṇas taken as prisoners. (11)

न तथा कटुघूत्कृताद् व्यथा मे हृदि जीर्णोपवनेषु घूकलोकात् ।
परिशीलित**पारसीक**वाग्भ्यो **यवनानां** भवने यथा शुकेभ्यः ।।१२।।

Screechings of owls in worn-out pleasure groves do not trouble me so much as the voice of parrots taught to speak Persian in the houses of Turuṣkas. (12)

स्तनचन्दनपाण्डु **ताम्रपणर्या**स्तरुणीनामभवत् पुरा यदम्भः ।
तदसूग्भिरुपैति शोणिमानं निहतानामभितो गवां नृशंसैः ।।१३।।

The waters of Tāmbraparṇī which were once white with sandal paste rubbed away from the breasts of charming young women are now flowing red with the blood of cows slaughtered by the miscreants. (13)

सुवते न यथापुरं वसुनि क्षितयो वर्षति पूर्ववन्न शक्रः ।
शमनोऽपि जनं नयत्यकाण्डे विषयेऽस्मिन् यवनैर्हतावशिष्टम् ।।१४।।

Earth is no longer the producer of wealth. Nor does Indra give timely intellect to it. The god of death takes his undue toll of what are left lives of undestroyed by the Yavanas. (14)

श्वसितानिलशोषिताधराणि श्लथशीर्णायतचूर्णकुन्तलानि ।
बहुबाष्पपरिप्लुतेक्षणानि **द्रमिडानां** वदनानि वीक्ष्य द्रये ।।१५।।

I am very much anxious by looking at the tearful faces of Draviḍa maids. Their lips parched by hot sighs and their hair tattered in utter disorder. (15)

श्रुतिरस्तमिता **नयः** प्रलीनो विरता धर्मकथा च्युतं चरित्रम् ।
सुकृतं गतमाभिजात्यमस्तं किमिवान्यत् कलिरेक एव धन्यः ।।१६।।

The Kali Age deserves now deepest congratulations for being at the peak of its power, for gone is sacred learning, hidden is refinement, hushed is the voice of *dharma*; destroyed is the discipline and discounted is the nobility of birth. (16)

इति सा निखिलं निवेद्य राज्ञे **यवनानां** जनगर्हितं चरित्रम् ।
अतिभीषणमात्मनः प्रभावात् कमपि प्रादुरभावयत् कृपाणम् ।।१७।।

Having thus narrated the sickening career of the Yavanas, she (the strange woman that appeared before Kampana) by his wonderful power of magic caused a terrible-looking sword to appear. (17)

अथ तं कलधौतकोश[तः सा क*]रलग्नत्सरुरुच्चखान खड्गम् ।
अचिरोज्झितकञ्चुकानुबन्धस्फुटकालोरगभोगसाम्यभाजम् ।।१८।।

In its shining silver sheath and handle, it looked like a serpent that had recently sloughed. (18)

क्षयकालकरालभद्रकालीगलकालागरुकर्द[मायमा*]नैः ।
महसां प्रसरैरदीपहार्यं किमपि ध्वान्तमिव प्रकाशयन्तम् ।।१९।।

In its darkish brilliance it resembled the *agāru* paste that one might imagine on the body of Bhadrakālī whose advent marks the end of this universe. (19)

प्रतिबिम्बितदीपकान्तिमन्तः स्फुटतापिञ्छतरुप्रसूननीलम् ।
नवमम्बुधरं विडम्बयन्तं जठरोज्जृम्भितवैद्युतप्रकाशम् ।।२०।।

With the images of burning lamps reflected in its surface, it looked like a fresh cloud bright with lightening within it. (20)

तमरातिनराधिनाथनारीनयनाम्भःकणपातहेतुभूतम् ।
प्रभुरुन्मिषितस्वरोषवह्नेरधिकोद्दाममममंस्त धूमदण्डम् ।।२१।।
(कलापकम् ।)

Thus sword, efficacious in drawing tears and sorrow from the eyes of enemies' spouses, she placed before the king, (21)

प्रणयागत**चोलपाण्ड्य**लक्ष्मीश्रवणेन्दीवरमालिकायमानम् ।
विरचय्य पुरः कृपाणमेषा पुनरप्याह पुरन्दराभमेनम् ।।२२।।

as if it were the personification of the prosperity of goddess of Coḷas and Pāṇḍyas and began to further address him thus. (22)

नरनाथ! पुरा कृपाणमेनं विरचय्याखिलदेवतायुधांशैः ।
उपदीकृतवान् पिनाकपाणेर्दनुजानां विजयाय विश्वकर्मा ।।२३।।

Oh king! in golden times, this sword was made by Viśvakarmā with the melted splinters of all divine weapons, and he gave it as a present to God Śiva for the destruction of *asuras*. (23)

अमुमुग्रतपःकृतप्रसादः प्रददौ **पाण्ड्यनृपाय** सोऽपि देवः ।
यमुपेत्य चिरेण तस्य वंश्याः पृथिवीमप्रतिशासनामशासन् ।।२४।।

And that God gave it as a boon to the Pāṇḍya king, pleased with his severe austerities. And his successors had it for a long time and were the unchallenged rulers of their earth. (24)

अथ कालवशेन **पाण्ड्यवंश्यान्** गतवीर्यानवधार्य कुम्भजन्मा ।
मनुजेश्वर! मण्डलाग्रमेनं भवते प्रेषितवान् महाभुजाय ।।२५।।

Sage Agastya, seeing that the Pāṇḍya race has lost its old virility by the wearing influence of time, has now sent this scimitar to you, oh powerful king! (25)

अमुना युधि दुःसहं महः स्यात् तव नैसर्गिकसाहसप्रवृत्तेः ।
ध्रुवमूष्मणि दारुणो दवाग्निः किमुतोच्चण्डसमीरसंस्तवेन ।।२६।।

You are by nature daring and wedded to risky endeavours. The possession of this weapon will make you formidable in the battle. Forest fire is terrible enough, and if high winds also assist it, who can estimate its all-consuming fierceness. (26)

अधिसङ्गरमस्य च प्रभावाद् भविता ते न कदापि सत्वसादः ।
असितोमरचक्रचापमुख्यैर्द्विषदस्त्रैर्वपुषो न चाभिषङ्गः ।।२७।।

By the wonderful virtue of being armed with this weapon you will never fail in the field of battle, nor would any harm result from enemy weapons such as sword, disc or bow. (27)

अमुमास्त्रकरालरश्मिपालीरचितालीकतटिच्छटाविलासम् ।
ध्रुवतस्तव चेष्टितुं पुरस्तान्न कृतान्तोऽपि भवत्यलं किमन्यैः ।।२८।।

As you wave this lightning-like sword in battle, not even the god of death can dare oppose you, let alone, others. (28)

अमुनाशु विशस्य दक्षिणस्यां **मधुरायां** पुरि कंसवन्नृशंसम् ।
यवनाधिपतिं बलोत्तरस्त्वं विदधीथाः स्फुटमच्युतावतारम् ।।२९।।

You do now proceed to southern Madhurā and destroy the cruel king of Yavanas who is the enemy of the world, like Śrī Kṛṣṇa killed the demonic Kaṁsa who once ruled there (viz. northern Madhurā). (29)

अनिदंप्रथमो हि धार्यतेऽसौ भवतान्यैर्मनसाप्यधारणीयः ।
भुवनत्रयरक्षणैकदीक्षाविधिशंसी कटकः (पदा?करा)म्बुजेन ।।३०।।

Not for the first time will now be wearing this bracelet on your hand, which has been (even on prior occasions) the emblem of your vow of protecting the three worlds, this bracelet none but you can wear. (30)

चलवेणिभिरुल्बणारुणाक्षैर्विपुलश्मश्रुभिरात्तसिंहनादैः ।
विकटभ्रुकुटीकरालफालैस्त्वरमाणस्तृणगात् (?)**तुलुष्कशीर्षैः** ।।३१।।

You will scatter the heads of Turuṣkas, heads with those swinging tufts, those blood-shot eyes, those ferocious beards and furious-browed foreheads. (31)

ग्रसतु प्रथनाह्वये दिनादौ प्रथमानो भवतः प्रतापसूर्यः ।
मधुपानमदप्रदोषरुढं **यवनीनां** स्मितचन्द्रिकाविकासम् ।।३२।।

May the sun of your prowess in battle wipe off the smile of moonlight from the faces of the drunken Yavana ladies. (32)

अविनीतिदवानलानुबन्धादधिकोन्मीलदघर्मघर्मजातम् ।
निहताहितलोहिताम्बुवर्षैर्नृप! निर्वापय तापमुर्वरायाः ।।३३।।

Dharma is in great distress by being now subjected to the scorching influence of the evil-natured Yavanas, and earth in consequence looks parched as it were and so you may by the rain of enemies blood, dispel the sufferings of earth. (33)

परिपन्थिकबन्धकन्धरान्तःस्रुतरक्तासवपूरपारणाभिः ।
कटपूतनभूतयातुधानानभितस्तर्पयतात् तवैष खड्गः ।।३४।।

May the sword of yours feast the evil spirits such as Kaṭa, Pūtanā and Yātudhāna with the blood flowing down from the headless trunks of your evil adversaries. (34)

दुरितैकपरं **तुलुष्कनाथं** द्रुतमुत्खाय जगत्त्रयैकशल्यम् ।
प्रतिरोपय **रामसेतु**मध्ये विजयस्तम्भशतानि बाहुशालिन्! ॥३५॥

May you erect many a pillar of triumph in the middle of Rāmasetu by destroying the Turuṣka lord who is wedded to nothing but evil doings and who therefore is to be regarded as the thorny shrubs of the three worlds. (35)

त्वयि नाथ! नियन्तृतां प्रपन्ने धृतवेगा स्थिरसेतुबन्धनेन ।
प्रथयत्वनुकूलयानलीलामचिरेणैव **कवेरजा**करेणुः ॥*३६॥

The Kāverī like a tamed female elephant will regain her normal course in the proper pace only when you become the supreme governor, oh your majesty! (36)

॥ [इति श्रीगङ्गादेव्या विरचिते मधुराविजयम्-
नाम्नि वीरकम्परायचरिते अष्टमः सर्गः ।*] ॥

Thus ends the eighth canto of the life of Vīra Kamparāya known as *Madhurāvijayam* composed by Śrī Gaṅgādevī.

* इतः परं दश पत्राणि तालपत्रादर्शात् विभ्रष्टानि ।

नवमः सर्गः

Canto 9

*.............फलकेन केचित् प्रत्यर्थिनां वञ्चितबाणवर्षाः ।
अलक्ष्यपातं युगपत् कृपाणैः कृत्ताखिलाङ्घ्रींस्तुरगा....म् ।।१।।

Within a moment, soldiers showered arrows on the opponent; if they neglected, they were about to be attacked by long swords. (1)

आसञ्जिताः कङ्कमुखैर्विमुच्य ....भुवनेषु पङ्क्तिः ।
आराच्चरन्त्या विरराज मृत्योरुत्तम्भिता तोरणमालिकेव ।।२।।

Without any signs of escaping from the swords ... the rows on earth fell down like the decorated festoons. (2)

कृत्ताः शशाङ्कार्धमुखैः पृषत्कैर्धनुष्मतां हास्तिकहस्तकाण्डाः ।
रक्तह्रदेषु न्यपतन् भुजङ्गाः पारीक्षितस्येव मखानलेषु ।।३।।

Bowmen severed the hands of elephant riders with *ardha-candra* (half-moon) arrows, and they fell down in the pool of blood in the battlefield like serpents in the sacrificial fire of Parīkṣita's son. (3)

मुक्ताफलैर्वीरकृपाणलेखाविभिन्नगन्धद्विपकुम्भमुक्तैः ।
रक्तारुणैस्तत्क्षणघट्टनोत्थस्फुलिङ्गसङ्घातमतिर्वितेने ।।४।।

Pearls from the broken heads of elephants in rut attacked by heroic warriors fell down; that blood stained pearls looked like sparks produced in sudden collision. (4)

यावत् कृपाणेन विपाट्य कुम्भं निवर्तते सत्वरमश्ववारः ।
तावद् गृहीत्वास्य तुरङ्गमङ्घ्र्योरास्फालयामास गजस्तमुर्व्याम् ।।५।।

No sooner did a horseman begin to return after having cut with his sword the frontal globe of an elephant than that elephant

---

* इतः पूर्वं शताधिकश्लोकविच्छेदसंभावनया सर्गसङ्ख्या न निश्चेतुं शक्या ।

was seen seizing his horse between his legs and compress him. (5)

निशाचराः केचन कुञ्जराणां कुम्भस्थलान्निस्सृतमास्रपूरम् ।
निष्ठ्यूतमुक्तामणयः सहर्षं चुचूषुरुत्पुष्करनालदण्डैः ।।६।।

The blood flowing from the wounded frontal globes of elephants was seen being drunk through their trunks by some night raiding evil spirits in great delight, spitting the pearls that also came with blood stream. (6)

जिघत्सयान्तः पतगैः प्रविष्टैः प्रस्पन्दमानं कुणपं द्विपस्य ।
समीपमासाद्य सजीवबुद्ध्या व्यसुं सतृष्णोऽपि जहौ सृगालः ।।७।।

Birds of prey with a view to taste the inner flesh entered into the body of a dead elephant making it quiver, jackals that mistook it for sign of life fled away; though they very much loved to feast on the body. (7)

चक्रैर्निकृत्तानि शिरांसि यावदाधोरणानां न पतन्त्यधस्तात् ।
अक्लिष्टशोभान्यवतंसहेतोस्तावत् प्रतीष्टानि निशाचरीभिः ।।८।।

Just as the heads cut by wheels were about to fall down, they were snatched away somewhat afresh with life by *rākṣasa* women who desired to wear them as wreaths, on their ears. (8)

करेण कश्चित् पदयोर्गृहीत्वा क्षिप्तं दवीयो वियति द्विपेन्द्रः ।
पतन्तमाच्छिन्नकृपाणयष्टिः प्रत्यैच्छदुच्चैर्दशनद्वयेन ।।९।।

A certain elephant having seized by the foot and thrown up a warrior with his trunk, wanted to catch him again, as he fell, down from his pair of tusks. (9)

क्षिप्तो गजेनोर्ध्वमसिद्वितीयः स्कन्धे निपत्यास्य पुरस्तरस्वी।
निपात्य चाधोरणमभ्यमित्रं गजाधिरोहः स्वयमेव जज्ञे ।।१०।।

A certain brave warrior thrown up by his enemy's elephant alighted on his back with his sword with which he dispatched the enemy rider and installed himself in his place. (10)

द्विषा सरोषेण पृषत्कवर्षैर्निषूदितः कोऽप्यमरत्वमेत्य ।
चकार तस्योपरि पुष्पवर्षं सहर्षमुद्धोषितचाटुवादः ॥११॥

A certain warrior, after having been killed by the flood of arrows of his angry enemy, became god and from his place in heaven rained flowers upon the latter praising his valour with genuine delight. (11)

कुन्तेन कश्चिद् द्विषता विभिन्नस्तथैव संश्लेषममुष्य यातः ।
भिन्दन्नुरस्तेन चमत्कृतोऽभूद् गुणेषु को मत्सरमादधाति ॥१२॥

A certain warrior was struck with a lance by his enemy, and by embracing the latter with the same lance sticking in his body, the other got wounded. This act evoked great admiration, Who is there not moved by real exhibition of brave behaviour? (12)

चिराय कौचित् कलहायमानावन्योन्यकौक्षेयककृत्तशीर्षौ ।
विमुक्तदेहौ तदनुक्षणेन ससौहृदौ दिव्यपुरीमयाताम् ॥१३॥

Two warriors, meeting in single combat, cut each other's head with their swords after a long fight; leaving their bodies there. They went up together at once to celestial regions as close friends. (13)

सङ्ग्रामवन्यामभितश्चरन्तो दर्पोद्धताः केचन राजसिंहाः ।
प्रत्यर्थिनां पार्थिवकुञ्जराणां शिरांस्यभिन्दन्नखरैः[खराग्रैः*॥१४॥]

Some royal warriors, like lions, wandered in the battlefield, and tore the heads of their enemies with their sharp nails as if the latter were opposing elephants. (14)

.... ।
....स्तस्य विरोधियोधान् दृष्ट्वा जहासेव पलायमानान् ॥१५॥

... enemy stared at it with fear thinking of running away. (15)

एकप्रहारेण सकङ्कटानामाधोरणानां करिणां च देहैः ।
द्विधा विभिन्नैरभितो विवेक्तुमीषत्करास्तस्य विमर्दमार्गाः ॥१६॥

* इतः परं पत्रद्वयं निर्लेखं दृश्यते ।

With one blow of his sword he (king) split in two elephants and their riders with their mail coat. Their bodies, lying mingled, gave but a slight clue for distinctive ranks of elephants from those of foot soldiers. (16)

कुम्भेषु भिन्दन् नृपतिर्द्विपेन्द्रान् मुक्ताफलैः शर्करिलान्तराभिः ।
प्रावर्तयद् रक्ततरङ्गिणीभिः परश्शताः संयति **ताम्रपर्णीः** ।।१७।।

The king, by crushing the elephants on their globes produced stream of blood-like river scattering the pearls on their heads which looked like sands. He got a thought, by looking at them, that there was not only one Tāmraparṇī River but several hundreds of Tāmraparṇīs were flowing. (17)

तेन द्विपास्तोमरिणा विभिन्नाः कुंभस्थलैरुज्झितमौक्तिकौघैः ।
क्रौञ्चस्य जह्नुर्गुहशक्तिघातप्रकीर्णहंसप्रकरस्य शोभाम् ।।१८।।

The heads of other elephants he pierced with his javelins, and pearls were strewn out from them. This reminded one of Subrahmaṇya boring a hole in the Cruñca mountain through which hosts of swans came out. (18)

रंहस्विनः स्वाभिमुखान् क्षितीन्द्रो मृगान् नखाग्रेण यथा तरक्षुः ।
प्रसह्य वक्षस्सु युधि प्रवीरान् क्षुण्णानकार्षीच्छुरिकामुखेन ।।१९।।

The alert king cut and wounded the bodies of those that opposed him, who caught in front of him like a hyena destroys a deer with the sharp nails. (19)

शूरस्तथा प्राहृत मुद्गरेण शिरस्त्रवन्ति द्विषतां शिरांसि ।
यथा विनिर्यन्नयनानि तानि मङ्क्षु न्यमाङ्क्षुः स्वशरीर एव ।।२०।।

The brave king pounded the turbaned heads of his enemies with his mace in such a way that the eyes which came out of the sockets sank again in their old places. (20)

[तस्मि*]न्निति व्यापृतहेतिजाते परापतन्त्यः परिपन्थिसेनाः ।
कल्पक्षयोदर्चिषि हव्यवाहे महाम्बुधेराप इवाशु ने[शुः*] ।।२१।।

When the king, thus began to destroy the ranks of his enemies along with their several weapons, the opposing army fled before him and disappeared like showering rains in the huge fires that started at the end of the universe (*pralaya*). (21)

न जामदग्न्येन न राघवेण तथा न भीमेन न चार्जुनेन ।
आपादितस्तेन यथा समीके हर्षो महर्षेः कलहप्रियस्य ।।२२।।

Not even Jamadagni, Rāma, Bhīma or Arjuna provided such amusement as the king did to that the lovers of quarrels – Sage (Nārada) always loved the sight of a good battle. (22)

तत**स्तुलुष्कान्** युधि[कान्दिशी*] कानालोक्य विष्फारित घोरशार्ङ्ग ।
कम्पक्षितीन्द्रं यवनाधिराजः प्रत्यग्रहीद् वृत्र इवामरेन्द्रम् ।।२३।।

Then seeing all his Turuṣka forces routed out in battle, the Yavana king, stringing his fearful bow, met the king Kampana in single combat even as Vṛtra did to the king of gods – Indra. (23)

तं वीरपाणाधिकपाटलाक्षं ललाटलक्ष्यभ्रुकुटीकरालम् ।
मदस्य रोषस्य च देहबन्धं संभेदमाशङ्कत वीरवर्गः ।।२४।।

The warriors regarded him as the personification of anger and intoxication, his eyes were red with the drink of Vīrapana, and the knitted brows on his forehead were fearful to look at. (24)

निरायता तस्य तुरङ्गवेगा वेणिर्मणिश्रेणिमती चकाशे ।
अमर्षवह्नेर्ज्वलनोन्मुखस्य धूमच्छटेव स्फुरितस्फुलिङ्गा ।।२५।।

His jewelled tuft in a line of constant brilliance as he rode on his fast horse looked like the headdress of his smoking anger which was about to blaze. (25)

आस्फाल्यमानस्य च तेन गाढं शार्ङ्गस्य मौर्वीनिनदश्चकार ।
चिरात् परित्यज्य तमुच्चलन्त्या जयश्रियो नूपुरघोषशङ्काम् ।।२६।।

The sound produced by his forceful stringing of the bow seemed as if it were radiated from the anklets of the goddess

* इयानेन तालपत्रादर्शः समुपलब्धः ।

of victory, who, after having abandoned him for long, was now returning to him in hurriedness. (26)

पराक्रमाधःकृत**चोलपाण्ड्यं वल्लाल**सम्पल्लतिकाकुठारम् ।
रणोन्मुखं **कम्पनृपो**ऽभ्यनन्दीद् वीरः **सुरत्राण**मुदग्रशौर्यः ।।२७।।

The brave king Kampana delighted in his having an opponent like the Suratrāṇa (Sultāna) who had by his valour reduced the Coḷas and Paṇḍyas and despoiled the wealth of Vīra Ballāla (Vallāla). (27)

आकर्णमाकृष्टशरासनौ तौ मिथः किरन्तौ विशिखानसङ्ख्यान् ।
वीरौ स्वबाहुद्रविणानुरूपमायोधनं मानधनौ व्यधाताम् ।।२८।।

The two proud opponents fought in a manner befitting the respective might of their arms, by showering arrows on each other with their bows bent up to their ears. (28)

बाणा निरस्ता **यवनेन** तस्मिन्नपाङ्गपाता इव वीरलक्ष्म्याः ।
कम्पेश्वरेणाप्यभिपारसीकं शराः कटाक्षा इव कालरात्रेः ।।२९।।

The king of the Yavana warded off the arrows let fly by King Kampana, which were like the side glances of the goddess of heroism. And the king, similarly checked the Pārasika's (Persian's) arrows which resembled the eye dart of Yama's sister. (29)

स **केरल**प्राणमरुद्भुजङ्गान् **वन्यावनीन्द्र**द्रुमदाववह्नीन् ।
अन्ध्रान्धकारक्षयतिग्मभासो बाणानमुञ्चद् **यवने** नरेन्द्रः ।।३०।।

King Kampana let fly against the Yavana king his arrows that had, like serpents drunk the life breaths of Keralas, like fire had consumed the lords of the Vanya kingdom and like sun had destroyed the dark Āndhra. (30)

क्षतानि यान्यस्य शरैः शरीरे चकार वीरस्य **तुलुष्कवीरः** ।
वितेनिरे तानि नखाङ्कशङ्कां जयश्रियो भोगसमुत्सुकायाः ।।३१।।

The scratches caused by the Yavana king's arrow on the person of King Kampana shone like the nail marks of the goddesses of victory that was so fervent to enjoy her privacy. (31)

उदग्रमग्रे **यवना**धिभर्तुः साक्षात्कलेर्मौलिमिवाशुगेन ।
स मङ्क्षु सार्धं जयकाङ्क्षितेन **ध्वाङ्क्षध्वजं** ध्वंसयति स्म धन्वी ।।३२।।

The crow banner of the Yavana king which looked like the typification of the crown of Kali Age was destroyed by King Kampana, and with that the formers hope of victory came to an end. (32)

अमर्षितस्याथ पृषत्कवर्षं विमुञ्चतो विद्विषतः शरेण ।
स कार्मुकज्यामलुनात् **तुलुष्क**राज्यश्रियो मङ्गलसूत्रकल्पाम् ।।३३।।

The king with his arrow, cut the bowstring of the Turuṣka, king who was, in his fury, showering arrows at the Turuṣka king. It looked like as if the knife was laid on the auspicious chord round the neck of the *rājyalakṣmī* (kingly prosperity) of the Turuṣkas. (33)

विहाय शार्ङ्गं धनुरिद्धरोष**स्तुलुष्क**[वीरस्त*]रवारिमुग्रम् ।
तुरङ्गपर्याणनिबद्धवर्धाविलम्बि(भिः?नं) सत्वरमुज्जहार ।।३४।।

The Turuṣka hero blazing with anger, then threw away his bow, and hastily drew out his terrible sword that was hanging on the side of his horse saddle. (34)

अथाग्रहीत् **कम्पनृप**स्तमेव कौक्षेयकं काल[करालरूपम् ।
व्या*]पादनार्थं **यवनेश्वरस्य** यः प्रेषितः प्राक् कलशोद्भवेन ।।३५।।

Unwavering to make an end of the Yavana king, King Kampana also armed himself with that sword which Agastya had sent him, and which looked as terrible as Yama himself. (35)

विषच्छटाधूम्ररुचिर्नृपस्य कराग्रधूता करवाललेखा ।
[जिह्वेव रेजे*] **यवनाधिराज**प्राणानिलाञ् जिग्रसिषोर्भुजाहेः ।।३६।।

That sword, grey-coloured like poisoned fumes as it was being waved by the hand of King Kampana, looked like a serpent about to drink the life breath from Yavana's body. (36)

स वञ्चयंस्तत्तरवारिधारां धाराविशेषप्रवणौपवाह्यः ।
अशातयत्तस्य शिरो निमेषा[दने*]न **कर्णाट**कुलप्रदीपः ।।३७।।

Seated on his lively horse, King Kampana, who was the glory of the Karṇāṭa race, avoiding the sword blow aimed by the Yavana, cut off in an instant the head of the Turuṣka. (37)

अज्ञातसेवोचितचाटुवादं **तुलुष्क**साम्राज्यकृताभिषेकम् ।
दिवौकसामप्यकृतप्रणामं भूमौ **सुरत्राण**शिरः पपात ।।३८।।

The head of the Suratrāṇa (Sultāna) fell on the ground, the head that never knew the art of persuading the servants, the head that had borne the royal burden of the Turuṣka kingdom, and had not bowed down even to gods. (38)

च्युतेऽपि शीर्षे चलिताश्ववल्गानियन्त्रणव्यापृतवामपाणिम् ।
प्रतिप्रहारप्रसृतान्यहस्तं वीरः कबन्धं द्विषतोऽभ्यनन्दीत् ।।३९।।

The hero Kampana was astonished to see that, even after the head had fallen the trunk on the horseback still held the reins, checking the horse's course with one hand, while the other was uplifted to return the blow of the enemy. (39)

मानोन्नते **कम्पनृपस्य** मौलौ पपात दिव्यद्रुमपुष्पवृष्टिः ।
स्वयंवराभ्युत्सुकराजलक्ष्मीविमुक्तमुक्ताक्षतजालकल्पा ।।४०।।

Then the head of King Kampana, held high in pride, fell heaps of flowers showered from the celestial regions and those heaps had the appearance of auspicious yellow rice (*akṣata*) sprayed by the goddesses of kingly prosperity, on herself choosing her lord. (40)

प्रशान्तदावेव वनान्तलक्ष्मीर्गतोपरागा गगनस्थलीव ।
कलिन्दजा मर्दितकालियेव दिग् दक्षिणासीत् क्षत**पारसीका** ।।४१।।

Like the beauty of the forest saved from forest fire, like the view of the sky after the completion of an eclipse, or like the calm appearance of the River Yamunā after the eradication of the serpent Kāliya the region of the south shined after the overthrow of Pārasikas. (41)

हतावशिष्टानथ वैरियोधान् संरक्ष्य पादप्रण*.......... ।
.... ।।४२।।

King Kamparāya assured the safety of the remaining men in his enemy ranks and was crowned with happiness and glory. (42)

।। [इति श्रीगङ्गादेव्या विरचितं मधुराविजयम्-
नाम्नि वीरकम्परायचरितं समाप्तम् ।*] ।।

Thus ends the ninth canto, of the life of Vīra Kamparāya known as *Madhurāvijayam* composed by Śrī Gaṅgādevī.

शिवं भूयात् ।

Conquest of Madurā

Text in Analysis

Prelude to the Plot of the Text

THE year 1336 CE in south Indian history is very popular and remarkable because it is the founding year of the Vijayanagara Empire, an event which almost at once changed the political scenario of the entire south in fourteenth century. Prior to 1336 CE the entire south India was under the domination of the ancient Hindu kingdoms; the Pāṇḍyas at Madhurā, the Coḷas at Tañjore and other small feudatories to the Pāṇḍyas and Coḷas. When Vijayanagara came into being the past was perpetual, and the monarchs of the new state became lords or overlords of the territories. This was the natural result of the persistent efforts made by the Muslims to conquer south India after their stabilization in north India. When these dismayed invaders reached the Kṛṣṇā River and attacked the Hindus in the south, who were stricken with terror, come together to create the new state of Vijayanagara which stood alone and offered some hope of protection from the Muslim attacks. From then on, the decayed old states crumbled away to nothingness, and the powerful kings of Vijayanagara became the saviours of the south for two and a half centuries.

The features of the Vijayanagara kingdom were manifold as follows.

On the banks of Tuṅgabhadrā River, Harihara Rāya built the city of Vijayanagara after the fall of the Hoyasaḷas of Kāmpilī, made it his capital, and founded the Vijayanagara empire. In the first half of the fourteenth century of the common era south India became disintegrated into pieces unable to withstand the Muslim attacks and the entire south up to Rāmeśvaram bounded by the sea fell into the Muslim hands. In the fort of Devagiri the supremacy of Rāmacandra Deva, Sevuna king, was taken over by Alauddin Khalji in 1295 CE and in 1314 CE after the death of Rāmacandra he merged the kingdom into the stronghold of the Delhi Empire. Malik Kafar's armies, raided the kingdoms of Dvārasamudram, Warangal and Madhurā. Though disabled and devoid of independence, these kingdoms somehow pulled on until the collapse of the Khalji dynasty. But with the emergence of the Tughlaq kingdom, in south India, again the days of oppression started. Muslim invasions increased. Hindu kingdoms were eventually wiped out and led to the establishment of the Tughlaq Empire. The Warangal fort of the Kākatīyas fell in 1323 CE. Later, all the seashore forts of the Āndhras were annexed by the Muslims. Even Malabar and Madhurā were snatched away from the Pāṇḍyas and were merged with the Delhi Empire. Even then invasions did not cease. In Karnataka, Hoyasaḷa and Kāmpilī kingdoms had yet to be subdued. Without conquering them, the emperors of Delhi could not have suzerainty over the entire south India.

Kāmpila, the founder of the Kāmpilī kingdom, having been originally in the service of Yādava Rāmacandra gained vast experience in the battle between Hoyasaḷas and his king, and on the capture of Rāmacandra by Malik Kafar and his removal from Delhi revolted against the Muslims. He waged war incessantly against the Muslims, refused to yield, established his kingdom and even extended it, by conquering a portion of it from the adjacent kingdom of Ballāla. So Malik Kafar, the commander of Alauddin Khalji, came upon Kāmpilarāya in the vain and returned back discomfited. Then onward, the Kāmpilī kingdom continued to be independent.

Kāmpilarāya gave shelter to Harihara and Bukka. Later they became ministers of Pratāparudra after the fall of the Kākatīya dynasty, and employed them in his own service. Bahauddin Gustasp, a relative of Sultan Mohammad-Bin-Tughlaq, rebelled against the Delhi Empire but was unfortunately defeated by the Delhi armies. So he sought refuge under Kāmpilarāya. Thus Kāmpila became a target to the wrath of the Delhi king. In spite of several invasions against Kāmpila, the latter successfully resisted and defeated the armies from Delhi. But at the end, during the siege of the fort of Hosapeṭ in 1327 CE Kāmpilarāya died. His sons, and the ministers Harihara and Bukka were taken as captives and were converted into Islam. At the fall of Kāmpilī, Bahauddin Gustasp took the shelter of Ballāla of the Hoyasaḷa kingdom. The armies of Delhi entered the Hoyasaḷa kingdom. Ballāla was incapable of resisting the Delhi forces. So he arrested Gustasp and surrendered him to the Delhi Sultan.

Mohammad-Bin-Tughlaq rejoiced over it, returned to Delhi without invading the Hoyasaḷa kingdom of Ballāla. By this, Tughlaq became the emperor of the entire Hindu India. With the conquest of the south India, his empire got extended from Peshawar in the west to Bay of Bengal in the east and from the Himalayas in the north to Setubandha the Rāmeśvaram in the south. But soon after, even his vast empire became disintegrated into pieces.

After the fall of the kingdom of Kāmpila, the Sultan stayed for two years in the south, to set right and consolidate or stabilize the administration, but, in 1329 CE he had to go back on account of the revolt in the Punjab. In the south the ruler of Kāmpilī town was subjected to several hardships. Neither paddy nor other commodities were allowed to reach the town. Hindu kings stopped paying tributes to him and put him to manifold difficulties. Unable to bear all this, the ruler sought the help of the Sultan at Delhi. The Sultan sent Harihara and Bukka the ministers of Kāmpilarāya, then in his captivity, for administering of the Kāmpila Deśa. They came to the south. But as they were converts into Islam and came on behalf of the Sultan, Ballāla did not accept their authority. They were defeated in the fight with Ballāla and fled to the nearby forest. But, by the grace of Sage Vidyāraṇya, who lived near the Pampāpāthi Temple in Hampī, they were again converted into Hindu religion, and resolved to drive out the Muslims and protect and revitalize Vedic Dharma, hence, the Vijayanagara emperors then on were known as *vaidikadharmapratiṣṭhāpanācārya*'s. Later with the help of Vidyāraṇya, they subdued Ballāla with Ānegoṇḍi as the capital, began to rule.

At this juncture, all the vigorous efforts made by the Delhi emperor to subdue the revolt of Jalaluddin, governor of Malabar, having failed, the prestige of the emperor waned and the trials to revive the Hindu kingdom gathered strength and momentum. Soon after the departure of the Sultan from the south, Kapayanāyakuḍu who succeeded Prolayanāyaka sought and obtained military help from Ballāla and defeated Malik Makbul, the ruler of Telaṅgānā in 1336 CE and captured

Warangal. Makbul fled to Delhi. Kapayanāyakuḍu assisted by Ballāḷa, entered Toṇḍaimaṇḍalam and drove away the Muslim armies belonging to Malabar, from there and entrusted that province to Śambhuvarāya. Thus the suzerainty of the Sultan ended in the south. In the Telugu land, not only the kingdom of Kapayanāyaka but also some other Hindu kingdoms sprang up. Koppulanāyakulu, with Pīṭhāpur as capital, ruled over the Kṛṣṇā and Godāvarī regions. The Reddy kings of Koṇḍaviḍu held sway over the region between Śrīśailam and the sea to its east, while the Velama kings began to reign in the Nalgoṇḍā area. In Tamil Nadu, the Toṇḍaimaṇḍalam or region under Sambhuvarāya, Coḷa and Pāṇḍya regions under the governor of Malabar became independent and defied the Sultan. Without letting loose this opportunity, Harihararāya and Bukkarāya began to expand their kingdoms with a view to revive and rehabilitate Hindu religion.

At the behest of Vidyāraṇya, they built Vidyānagara in 1336 CE as capital and while Harihararāya was effectively administering the kingdom, Bukkarāya under the able guidance of his minister Mādhava extended the kingdom as far as the sea on the east, this expansion has furnished sufficient power and financial stability. By then, on the west, the Hoyasaḷa kingdom under the third Ballāla became an obstacle to the growth of the Vijayanagara Empire on account of its firmness and expansion. So Bukkarāya gradually began to invade the Hoyasaḷa kingdom. In 1340 CE, he could seize the Kukkalanāḍu region, to his kingdom. But Ballāla reconquered it and protected his kingdom till 1342 CE when in the war he waged against the Sultan of Madhurā and Ballāla III died at the hands of Ghiyasuddin during his raid against Tiruchirapalli. Being aware of this unprotected state of the Hoyasaḷas, Bukkarāya, then ruling over Udayagiri and Gutti invaded and conquered the fort at Penugoṇḍa. Gradually even by the next year, he subdued Hosapaṭnam and Dvārasamudram and the Mūlubagal region of present-day Kolar district of Karnataka and also drove away Ballāla IV from the Hoyasaḷa and annexed it to the Vijayanagara Empire. Despite all this victory of Harihararāya and Bukkarāya, Hindu religion was destroyed by the Sultan of Delhi and the Muslim rulers of Madhurā. All Hindus were subjected to series of miseries. Many temples were destroyed. All people were reduced to slavery. There was no scope for the development of fine arts, culture and Vedic Dharma, as all these were suppressed ruthlessly beyond recognition. In such critical time, Kampana, the son of Bukka came on the scene, retrieved Hindu religion, gave protection to the people and struggled for the prosperity of the country.

It is here in this background the text of *Madhurāvijayam* (*MV*) or the life of Vīra Kamparāya can be situated. This *mahākāvya* was written by the queen and the chief consort of King Kumāra Kampana and hence here it is essential to throw light on the political scenario of south India in the first half of the fourteenth century before analysing the contents of the text and also it is relevant to discuss the political condition which made Vīra Kamparāya to fight war against Muslims and also with the Tamil king of Madhurā. The account mentioned and gathered may or may not be accurate in all details, but it at least tallies fairly with the epigraphical and other records of the time.

Thus the period at which the plot of *Madhurāvijayam* opens, about the year 1365 CE, found the whole of north India down to the Vindhya mountains firmly under Muslim rule, while the followers of that faith had overrun the deccan and were threatening the south with the same fate. South of the Kr̥ṣṇā the whole country was still under Hindu domination, but the supremacy of the old dynasties was shaken to its base by the rapidly advancing terror from the north.

This Kampana popularly known as Vīra Kampana Oḍeyar, husband of Gaṅgādevī, is the hero of the present poem, which is considered as a *mahākāvya* and also as *carita*. Since he is the hero of the present poem, it documents his birth and other life events. However, being considered as a *mahākāvya* it tends to be one of the characters of *mahākāvya* writings – the life of an important person such as a king has to be potrayed and also this poem is one of the poems which is considered as a historical poem of India of the nineteenth century.[1] In

---

[1] It is defined that the history of Indians combines itself not only an account of past events, but also many important instructions or advices on the four goals of life, such as *dharma*, *artha*, *kāma* and *mokṣa*. History to Indians is just a means through which the inculcation in posterity of the fourfold object of life is to be attempted. That, the Europeans blaming Indians as totally lacking historical sense, is unreasonable. There have been *nārāsaṁśī*s and *gāthā*s; the seeds of historical writing were even in the earliest literature such as the Vedas. The real cause that prevented the growth of strictly historical literature,

→

the nineteenth century, some European scholars contended that India had no records of history. To counter their claims, this poem is of great help and it thus occupies pride of place as being classed as a historical poem and the contents of it are declared to be the part of history which will be discussed at length. Along with this poem Kalhaṇa's *Rājataraṅgiṇī*, Bāṇa's *Harṣacarita*, Bilhaṇa's *Vikramāṅkadevacarita*, Daṇḍin's *Daśakumaracaritam* were considered as historical works. But, there is good deal in all such works which does not befit the nature of correct history. In this respect, *Madhurāvijayam* has been regarded as an important literary source in the reconstruction of the past history of India. No doubt, the writing of India's past history in the frame of literature is not an easy task. The literature more often sprinkles some bits of meagre history which may substantiate on the basis of a pre-conceived history. Therefore, there was a need to develop on objective outlook on the part of historians. It is *Madhurāvijayam* that fulfils the need; as such, it has been important work which corroborates with epigraphy and numismatics.

But *Madhurāvijayam* occupies place of pride as not only it is a historical poem but also as the poem authored by a woman – poetess. This poem was first edited in 1924 by Harihara Śāstrī. Since then there were many studies of this text, historical as well as literary. This text is considered as a primary source of the history of Saṅgama dynasty of Vijayanagara empire. Hence it has been translated into all the south Indian languages – Tamil, Telugu and Kannada and also into English more than once.

Analysis of Text in Its Contents

Madhurāvijayam of Gaṅgādevī runs into 521 verses which have been divided into the nine cantos and is structured in *dvipada* style. The total number of verses in *Madhurāvijayam* may differ from edition to edition, as there are additions and deletions of verses. All the nine cantos have been set with beautiful and lucid words, as well as strong language. But the text, as mentioned above, gives some valuable

← in modern sense in Sanskrit, is the different attitude of Indians towards life as a whole other than Europeans or any outsider. We can collect rich historical elements of different phases from the Vedic literature. But the history that we find here is generally mixed with myths and legends, characteristic of India.

historical information which is even corroborated by epigraphical and archaeological and other sources. Gaṅgādevī herself says:

> Learned men, please listen therefore to this poem of mine dealing with the life of King Kampana going by the famous title of the conquest of Madhurā. – *MV* 1.25

Then what history *Madhurāvijayam* tells us? The text starts with prayers to the Gaṇeśa and remembering Śaivite and Vaiṣṇavite gods along with famous poets preceding and contemporary to the poetess. Later it sketches and depicts Kamparāya's life introducing her father Bukka and his elder brother Harihara, thereafter follows all other events in the life of hero Kumāra Kampana.

But, so far as *Madhurāvijayam* is concerned, there is no scope for controversy to the fact that Bukka was the real successor.[2] According to the epigraphic accounts of 1356 CE, Bukka succeeded his brother Harihara I to the throne of Vijayanagara. Already, he had been well acquainted with the problems of the new kingdom. In fact, he was an efficient ruler in the administration of different regions of the kingdom. After obtaining the crown, he set himself to the task of getting rid of the hostile elements and consolidating the new kingdom. He was a kṣatriya. This is borne out by the propriety of various descriptions of this *kāvya*. Poem equates him with Indra and Kubera, also with Yama.

> He established the existence of the (four) guardian deities of the universe even on this earth, by being victorious (like Indra), by being the overlord of the waters (like Varuṇa), by giving away wealth (like Kubera) and by being impartial (like Yama). – *MV* 1.30

He is the most renowned of all the kings of the Saṅgama dynasty of Vijayanagara. Some inscriptions clearly say that Bukka had enjoyed a great honour of having various titles like *mahāmaṇḍaleśa*, *vibhāḍa*, *rājādhirāja* and *rājaparameśvara*. He has adorned the crown of fame which is described as the lord of eastern and western oceans as may be seen from another inscription. He is compared with Arjuna and described as he drove out the enemies from many royal cities and ruled

---

2 There was a famous king called Bukka who was the younger brother of Harihara and whose orders were abided by the kings of all the neighbouring vassals. – *MV* 1.26

over an empire perfecting them in seven parts. However, King Bukka as stated in *Madhurāvijayam* has three sons by his queen, Devāyī, viz. (Hiriya), Kampana (Cikka), Kampana and Saṅgama.

> Then in course of time the queen bore to the king two other sons called Kampana and Saṅgama who were like *pārijāta* and *cintāmaṇi* that sprang from the milky ocean. – *MV* 2.40

The *Madhurāvijayam* states that Bukka I named his first son Kampana, because after his birth, the enemies of Vijayanagara began to shake with fear and also this is the name of his grandfather Kāmpila or Kampa the chief and founder of Kāmpila kingdom which after the reign of Saṅgama merged into the newly-founded Vijayanagara kingdom.[3]

> The king who constantly looked ahead named his child Kampana as he clearly foresaw in his mind that in proper time the later would become a matchless warrior. And was sure to make his enemies in the field of battle quake with fear. –*MV* 2.34

However, an inscription from Kolar, praises Kampana in the following words:

> A sun unbounded valour, a moon incarnate in serenity, a unique treasure of music, a tree of paradise to the learned, intent upon establishing *dharma*, Lord of the Goddess of Sovereignty with a name renowned among kings, was Vīra Kumāra Kampāna.
> –*Epigraphia Carnatica*, vol. X, Kolar no. 222, dated 8 February 1356

The text, after recording the birth and childhood of Kampana in detail, introduces his father Bukka and his relation. Kampana was entrusted by his father with the task of extending the Vijayanagara rule to the Tamil country. In the reign of Bukka I, Yuvarāja Kampana (Hiriya) was requested by his father to undertake an expedition over the south, when he was the governor of "Mulubāgilu-rājya".

> So you better march successfully to Tuṇḍīra (Toṇḍaimaṇḍalam) and overcome the people headed by the Campa (Śambhuvarāya) who are preparing for war. Then establish yourself at Kāñcī and rule there, with due regard to the wishes of the people even like the Lord of Wealth (Kubera) does in the city of Alakā. Then if you subdue all

[3] This is one of the legends on the foundation and formation of early Vijayanagara Empire.

> the Vanya kings it would be easy for you to break the power of the Turuṣkas. Would it be difficult for the fire, that had consumed with its flames hundreds of branches of a tree, to destroy the trunk? This Turuṣkas is acting like Rāvaṇa in regard to the southern kingdoms. If you play the part praise worthy of Śrī Rāma in reducing him, you will be rendering a service to the world and relieve sufferings.
>
> – *MV* 3.41-43

As a first step in this direction, he invaded the territories of Śāṁbhuvarāya of Rājagambhīra-rājya. Kampana succeeded in capturing the fort and taking prisoner the rebellious chief Rājanārāyaṇa. Rājagambhīra-rājya meant the annexation of the North and South Arcot and Chinglepet districts. As stated by Gaṅgādevī, Bukka I advised his son Kumāra Kampana to march against the Śambhuvarāya. Chieftain, of Padaivīḍu in Toṇḍaimaṇḍalam to defeat him in the battle and then to establish himself at Kāñcī.

> So, I would ask you to exhibit your manliness and ever-increasing prowess and strike at your enemies and subdue them, even as the Lord of the Gods (Indra) did in the case of the (winged) mountains enraged at their efforts to destroy the world. – *MV*

At this juncture, it should not be forgotten that the history of the Tamil country refers to two great Śambhuvarāya rulers – Venrumankoṇḍa Śambhuvarāya (1321-39 CE) and his son Rājanārāyaṇa Śambhuvarāya. (*c.*1339-63). Here, a doubt arises as to who was the Śambhuvarāya. that came into conflict with and defeated by Kampana of Vijayanagara. It has been an admitted fact that Kampana's conquests over different territories took place after 1340 CE. Venrumankoṇḍa Śambhuvarāya flourished before the reign of Kampana and the date of Rājanārāyaṇa Śambhuvarāya goes well with that of Kampana. A. Krishnaswami Aiyangar asserts – the inscription from Madampakkam dated 1363 CE simply mentions that Gandaragali Marayya Nāyaka, the general of Kumāra Kampana captured the Venrumankoṇḍa Śambhuvarāya occupied Rājagambhīramalai. Does this name Venrumankoṇḍa Śambhuvarāya in any way suggest that he was the son and successor of Rājanārāyaṇa? The fact seems to be that Rājanārāyaṇa himself is referred to the record as "Venrumankoṇḍan" assumed by his father. Therefore, it was Rājanārāyaṇa Śambhuvarāya who was defeated by

Kumāra Kampana. But the above inscriptional evidence disproves the statement of Gaṅgādevī that the Śambhuvarāya was killed in a duel with Kumāra Kampana.[4] However, Gaṅgādevī gives no date of the conquest of Toṇḍaimaṇḍalam ruled over by Rājanārāyaṇa Śambhuvarāya, by Kumāra Kampana. For this, one should rely on the inscriptional evidence. It is already known that Rājanārāyaṇa Śambhuvarāya ruled over Toṇḍaimaṇḍalam, from 1336 CE and lived up to 1363 CE. His last regnal record, from Ukkal – in North Arcot district bears the date of Śaka 1284, to the 26th year of Rājanārāyaṇa's rule and yields correct date of 30 March 1362 CE. No inscription of Rājanārāyaṇa Śambhuvarāya, mentioning him as a ruler, after that date, is so far available. Two other inscriptions of Kumāra Kampana enable us to determine the date of the conquest with some accuracy. They are available from Serkāḍu in North Arcot district and both of them are dated 3 January 1363 CE. They registered the free colonization of the temple, the people and the order of Kumāra Kampana that the taxes collected from them should be for worship and repairs of the temple of Serkāḍu. This was done at the instance of Mahā Pradhānī Somappā Oḍeya for the continuity of Kampana's rule. It is clear from these two records that Kampana's rule was established in the Śambhuvarāya's territory before 3 January 1363 CE. Hence the nearest approximate date of the conquest may be fixed between October and December 1362, CE.

After conquering the Draviḍa king, Prince Kampana proceeded to Kāñcī. Then he began to rule at Tuṇḍīramaṇḍala. An inscription of Kampana dated Śaka 1287 found in Tirupputkuli near Kāñcī records that Bukkanna Udaiyara's son Kampana Udaiyar became established on the "throne after taking possession of the Rājagambhīra-rajya". When he was returning from Kāñcīpuram he was described as a *samrāṭ* (emperor). He won the hearts of the people there. It also indicates the same that is as part of the scheme as mentioned in *Madhurāvijayam*. His subjects had considered him as another incarnation of Viṣṇu and his fame, spread far and wide, after establishing himself at Kāñcī.

The fourth canto of *Madhurāvijayam* deals with the details of Kampana's marching against the forces of the Śambhuvarāya. The

[4] Then escaping skilfully a sword plunge, King Kampana dispatched the Śambuvarāya (monarch) as a guest to Indra's city. – *MV* 4.82

ending portion of this canto states that Kumāra Kampana arriving with his army at Viriñcīpuram attached the forces of Śambhuvarāya which were then completely defeated and Śambhuvarāya took refuge at the hill fortress called Rājagambhīramalai. But the fortress was besieged. Being unable to stand the siege for a long time, Śambhuvarāya came out of the fort with sword in hand. Then a duel took place between them. In that duel Kampana killed Śambuvarāya.

> Kampana's sword, reflecting as it did, the image of the Śambuvarāya monarch, looked like a pregnant daughter about to give birth to a husband for the celestial nymphs. Then escaping skilfully a sword plunge, King Kampana dispatched the Śambuvarāya (monarch) as a guest to Indra's city. – *MV* 4.81-82

> Having thus reduced the Śambhuvarāya in the field of battle, King Kampana received the decree of his father that he should rule the territory thus conquered, with the fame of his victory duly established in Kāñci, he inaugurated a just and prosperous rule over Tuṇḍīramaṇḍala destroying all terminations in castes and religious orders. – *MV* 4.83

> His accomplished system of light taxation pleased his subjects of his kingdom, and earth herself showed a great satisfaction by her excellent yield of corn and other produce. – *MV* 5.5

The concluding canto of *Madhurāvijayam* describes at full length the battle between the forces of Kumāra Kampana and the Sultan of Madhurā. Kumāra Kampana next proceeded further south against the Sultanate of Madurai, which was established in 1334 CE by Jalaluddin-Hasan Shah, who had been in continuous warfare with the Hoysaḷas. Hoysaḷa king Ballāla III had lost his life while fighting with the Sultan of Madurai. This Sultanate of Madurai proved a source of endless annoyance and distress to the people of the region. *Madhurāvijayam* describes the condition of Madurai in the following words.

> Where there resounded once the joyous sound of the *mṛdaṅgam* there at present heard the howl of the jackal that has made it its abode. The River Kāverī that had been regulated by proper dams and flowed into regular channels has began to flow in all directions. In the Agrahāras where the *yāga*s and *homa*s were largely visible and the sound of the chanting of the Vedas was everywhere heard, we

> have now the offensive smelling smoke issuing from the roasting of flesh by the Muslims and their harsh voice alone to hear, the beautiful coconut trees which were gracing the gardens surrounding the city of Madhurā have been cut down and in their place we see plenty of *śūla*s-tridents, with garlands made by stringing human heads together resembling in a remote manner, the coconut trees. The waters of the River Tāmraparṇī which used to be white with sandle paste rubbed away from the breasts of the young and beautiful maidens, who were bathing in it, is now flowing red with the blood of brāhmaṇas and cows slaughtered by the Muslims.[5] – *MV* 7.1-8

After having described the pitiable conditions of the Tamil country as above, the mysterious lady was said to have presented Kumāra Kampana with a divine sword and ordered him to proceed against the Sultan of Madhurā who was the enemy of the world. This description of the condition of the temples and the people, though poetic in character, cannot be regarded as opposed to facts of history. Ibn-Battuta and the Hindu chronicles paint equally horrible pictures of the rule of the

[5] Even though Gaṅgādevī's observations seem exaggerated, nonetheless the Muslim rule was unfamiliar to the Tamil people. It was against their religious fervour and the attempts to convert religious faiths of the people had an impact on the public order. The people were longing to be freed from the clutches of the Muslim yoke. This made them to welcome the Vijayanagara rulers who were emerging as the benefactors of Hindus and Hinduism. It is to be noted that the immediate task at that time was to restore the social and religious order of the day. This was done by the viceroys of Vijayanagara to an extent till the end of their rule. But as an invader, Kumāra Kampana crowned himself and did not restore the sceptre to its legitimate Hindu Pāṇḍya ruler. To the Tamils it meant only a change of masters. Tamil Nadu came under another alien empire, i.e. under the Kannada–Telugu Hindu masters. They carried out many charitable endowments and rituals to keep the people under their control. They patronized the brāhmaṇas and restored temple paramountacy and caste-based sectionalism. Besides, their attitude was to expand their kingdom and to keep the people under their control. At the dawn of the sixteenth century, almost all parts of Tamil Nadu came under the control of the Mahāmaṇḍaleśvaras, later known as Nāyakas.They kept their own courts, levied taxes and issued coins and maintained an armed establishment.With the fall of Muslim Sultanate of Madurai, the Muslims moved to the coasts. From then onwards it is important in the history of Tamil Nadu that the Muslims started gaining control over the Fishery Coast.

Sultans of Madhurā and difficulties which the people had to experience.

Here in this connection Gaṅgādevī, wife of Kumara Kampana, narrates her husband's successful conquest over the Sultanate of Madurai.[6] After Rājagambhīrarājya and Koṅgudeśa came under his control, Kumāra Kampana turned his attention towards Madurai. According to *Madhurāvijayam* of Gaṅgādevī the Sultan of Madurai[7] was defeated by Kampana in a bloody battle near Madurai.

> The brave king Kampana, delighted in his having an opponent like the Suratrāṇa (Sultan) who had by his valour reduced the Coḷas and Pāṇḍyas and despoiled the wealth of Vīra Ballāla (Vallāla).
>
> – *MV* 9.25

> Unwavering to make an end of the Yavana king, King Kampana also armed himself with that sword which Agastya had sent him, and which looked as terrible as Yama himself. That sword, grey-coloured like poisoned fumes as it was being waved by the hand of King Kampana, looked like a serpent about to drink the life breath from Yavana's body. Seated on his lively horse, King Kampana, who was the glory of the Karṇāṭa race, avoiding the sword blow aimed by the Yavana, cut off in an instant the head of the Turuṣka. The head of the Suratrāṇa (Sultan) fell on the ground, the head that never knew the art of persuading the servants, the head that had borne the royal burden of the Turuṣka kingdom, and had not bowed down even to gods.[8]
>
> – *MV* 9.33-36

---

[6] Kumāra Kampana's conquest, of Tamil country in 1365 CE is also mentioned in the inscription on the Mīnākṣī Temple. The shrine was built four years before the conquest of Kumāra Kampana. It was the second Muslim conquest that took place which was described to be an uneventful one. On accepting the view of some scholars who hold 1370-74 CE as the year of Kumāra Kampana's conquest, it can be said that Gaṅgādevī has written *Madhurāvijayam* after the conquest of her husband Kampana. It may be taken a note of the opinion of that *Madhurāvijayam* has been composed by Gaṅgādevī during 1375-77 CE.

[7] Is this sultan Fakruddin Mubarak Shah?

[8] *Madhurāvijayam* does not refer to the name of the Sultan of Madhurā, who was defeated by Kampana. Yet the history of the Tamil Nadu does not throw light on the identification of the Sultan of Madhurā who was defeated by Kampana. Despite the chronological list of Sultans of Madhurā; the existence of coins cannot be denied as an imaginary one. Some of there coins mention →

This victorious army was assisted by his able generals, i.e. Saḷuva Maṅgu, Somayyā Daṇḍanāyaka, Viṭṭappā and Gopanna. But it is said that Saḷuva Maṅgu was killed by the Sultan. By 1371 CE the Madurai region became a part of the Vijayanagara empire and Kampana administered the Tamil country as the viceroy of Vijayanagara. The liberation of Madurai from Muslim rule soon resulted in the destruction of the garrisons of the Sultan stationed at other places. Gopanna conquered Śrīraṅgam.[9]

The temple of Raṅganātha had been neglected during Muslim rule; so it was renovated and the idol of Raṅganātha was said to be reinstalled by Gopanna, general of Kumāra Kampana.

> This means it is like Vyāghrapuri (*śloka* damaged – incomplete). In Śrīraṅgam the lord of serpents is seen warding off the tumbling debris of bricks with his hood in case they fall and disturb the sleep of *yoga* in which Hari is enfolded there. When I looked at the state of the temples of other gods, my distress knows no bounds. The breakdowns of their door are eaten up by termites. The arches over their inner shelters are let out with wild growth of vegetation. Those temples which were once resonant with the melody of *mṛdaṅga* drums are now echoing the fearful howls of jackals. The River Kāverī, uncurbed by proper *bāndha*s (dams), has become deflected very much from her time honoured course, and flows in all sorts of wrong directions as if imitating the Turuṣkas in their actions. The brāhmaṇa streets, where

---

← three Sultans: (1) Adil Shah, (2) Fakhruddin Mubarak Shah, and (3) Allauddin Sikandar Shah. Of these three Sultans, who could be the person defeated by Kumāra Kampana? As has already been maintained, the date of the conquest of Madhurā by Kampana to be the April or May 1371 CE, it may be decided whether it was Fakhruddin Mubarak Shah for whom there are a number of coins dated AH 761 to 770, i.e. 1359 to 1370 CE. If the numismatic evidence is to be believed, the Sultan defeated by Kampana must be Fakhruddin Mubarak Shah. Because the coins of his successor are dated up to 1378 CE, when Kumāra Kampana was not alive. Thus it was Fakhruddin Mubarak Shah who was defeated by Kampana in 1371 CE. So it may be undoubtedly taken for granted that Fakhruddin Mubarak Shah was the Sultan defeated by Kumāra Kampana and took the possession of Madhurā.

[9] This is according to the information gathered from secondary sources on Vijayanagara history.

> once the sacrificial smoke was ever seen rising, and the chanting of Vedas always greeted the ears, now exclude the musty odour of meat, and resound with the lion-like roars of the drunken Turuṣkas.
>
> – *MV* 8.1-6

Gaṅgādevī in her *Madhurāvijayam* has added information to the stock of southern history. But the two sons of Bukka I, having the same name, have produced great confusion and difficulty in the already fused state of genealogy of the first Vijayanagara dynasty. The name Kampana is addressed to both the sons of Bukka I. However from the inscriptions available from Madras presidency and Mysore state, it is understood that the elder was called as Hiriya and the younger was called Cikka. However, some of the epigraphists of Madras assign that Kumāra Kampana was Cikka Kampana. Vīrabukkarāya Kampana and all those prefixes like Hiriya before the name Kampana, are assigned to his paternal uncle, Kampana. Anyhow, it can be derived that Bukka I, had two sons having the same name Kampana. But his first son popularly known as Hiriya Kampana invaded Madurai, this son of Bukka I bore the titles of *mahāmaṇḍaleśvara*, "Great lord of *maṇḍala*s" "subduer of hostile kings" and "lord of the four oceans". His influence had extended from Mysore in the north to Rāmanāḍa in the south.

To the south and west, conquests were more successful. Under Bukka I (r. 1344-77), Madurai was freed from the control of Muslim rebel commanders who declared a sultanate independent of the Tughlaqs in 1334. The Vijayanagara campaign against them was carried out between 1365 and 1370 by Bukka I's son Kumāra Kampana and was as much a propaganda as a military success because it was memorialized in numerous inscriptions over the southern peninsula proclaiming a new dhārmic kingship and an end to Muslim oppression.[10]

Vidyānagara or Vijayanagara

The city was known by several names besides Vijayanagara, which is hardly surprising since the earliest inscription from the place in Brāhmī

---

[10] King Kampana being a pious Hindu must have had a holy bath at Rāmeśvaram after his victory over Madhurā and made some gifts to the temple. The earliest of these inscriptions is dated Virodhikrtu Saṁvatsara, 8th Vaiśākhī, which is equivalent to 4 June 1371. Hence the battle of Madhurā may be considered to have taken place in April or May 1371.

script dates to about the second century CE. From the eleventh to the thirteenth centuries, several other inscriptions are found, including one registering gifts made to the temple of the Goddess Hampādevī (or Pampādevī) from which the modern village on the ruins of the city, Hampī, presumably comes. Hoysaḷa-period inscriptions refer to the place as Virūpākṣapaṭṭaṇṇa or Vijaya Virūpākṣapura in honour of God Śiva as Virūpākṣa, the protector of the large settlement of the place in the fourteenth century. These pre-Vijayanagara references make it clear that the future capital of the Vijayanagara kingdom was one of the many places in modern Bellary with a past history dating to Mauryan times when Aśokan edicts were inscribed within thirty miles of Hampī, along the banks of River Tuṅgabhadrā.

Text Considered as Mahākāvya and also as Carita

Rājaśekhara, the author of the *Kāvya-Mīmāṁsā* holds the view that literature is of two types, viz. *śāstra* and *kāvya*. While the former is a product of *prajñā,* the latter is of *pratibhā*. Both are like two paths of Sarasvatī, the goddess of learning. While *śāstra* is for hard-brained people, *kāvya* is for *sukumāramati*s – aestheticians as rightly said by Viśvanātha in his *Sāhityadarpaṇa*. The distinctive feature of *kāvya* is:

> "*niyatikr̥taniyamarahita, āhlādaikamayī ananyaparatantra, navarasarucird*"

As specified by Mammaṭa in his *Kāvya-Prakāśa*, The *kāvya* is therefore flowing like the River Ganges regularly from the time immemorial. In Sanskrit the poetical works are of four main varieties, viz.: *mahākāvya* (great poem, court epic), *khaṇḍa-kāvya* (shorter poem), *laghu-kāvya* (short-poem) and *muktaka-kāvya* (free verses). Viśvanātha in the *Sāhityadarpaṇa* has said about the following purposes of *kāvya*.

> Poetry brings fame and riches, knowledge of the ways of the world and relief from evils along with instant and perfect happiness and counsel sweet as from the tips of a beloved consort.

The entire corpus of this *mahākāvya* invariably consists of descriptions and narrations. Since technically the *mahākāvya* is of the *prabandha* type, narration has occupied an important position in it; otherwise, it was not possible to maintain the string of the story. But at the same time, the poetic faculty of the author of a *mahākāvya* cannot find its fulfilment merely by narrating a series of events or incidents. So, she has invariably created opportunities for introducing lengthy descriptions of objects which are grand, majestic and beautiful. It is, at times, very difficult to draw a line of demarcation between the narrations and the descriptions.

So far as the present *mahākāvya* is concerned, we can distinguish narrations from descriptions on the basis of the approach of the poetess. Those portions of this *mahākāvya* which narrate the various events of the story and also those, which tend to carry the *kathā-vastu* or plot of *mahākāvya* further and serve as a connecting link between what precedes it and what follows it, should be counted as narrations. There is no doubt that narration holds a subordinate position in *mahākāvya*, the major portion being occupied by descriptions. The method of narrative skill in this work has semblance with that in the *Raghuvaṁśa* of Kālidāsa, and the *Kirātārajunīyam* of Bhāravi, the *Śiśupālavadha* of Māgha, the *Rāmāyaṇa* of Vālmīki, i.e. because as the poetess states she has well read these authors of the poems and also imparted some ideas from them.

Gaṅgādevī's *Madhurāvijayam* is a *mahākāvya* in which descriptions occupy a major portion as compared to narrations. The narrations are very brief and are presented in a summarized form. It consists of all fundamental characteristics of the *mahākāvya*. However, she, in the opening section of the first canto, criticizes the persons who do not realize the importance of poetry and praises the *sahṛdaya*s.

The *Madhurāvijayam* of Gaṅgādevī has been one of the good poetries identified and accepted as the *mahākāvya*s. As she says she follows the poet Viśvanātha, hence, she adopts his characterization of *mahākāvya* such as:

1. The *mahākāvya* should run into the *sarga*s. It should consists of the *sarga*s (cantos) not less than eight, but not more than thirty. Each canto has a uniform metre, which may get changed at the end of the canto. The end of the canto should suggest the subject matter of the next canto.
2. The *mahākāvya* should begin with an auspicious benediction.
3. It should deal with the life of a single hero, or of many kings belonging to the same race. If the hero is only one he must be

either celestial, or a kṣatriya of noble family, and possessed of the qualities of *dhīrodātta* – generous and heroic type.

4. Any one of the sentiments of Śṛṅgāra, Vīra, Śānta and Karuṇa should be predominant in the *mahākāvya* and the rest of the nine sentiments (navarasa) remain as subordinate.
5. At least, one of the four goals of life should be addressed.
6. Denouncement of wicked ones and the praise of noble ones should be there.
7. It should consist of the description of a city, sea, mountains, seasons, sunrise, moonrise, garden, water sport, marriage, separation of lovers, birth of a son, sending the messengers and war.
8. It should be embellished with rhetorical figures of speech, sentiments and good style.[11]

Madhurāvijayam begins with an auspicious benediction in the form of salution of God Gaṇapati.

This *kāvya* deals with the life history of King Kampana belonging to warrior class. King Kampana himself is the hero of this *kāvya* and does possess the qualities of *dhīrodātta* type. He is said to be kind enough to the subjects, well-versed in all sciences, brave, handsome interested in philosophical discourses, strict in administration, etc.

In *Madhurāvijayam*, Vīra Rasa is predominant and sentiments like Śṛṅgāra (cantos II, V), Bhayānaka and Bībhatsa (Canto V) Rasas have been subordinately entertained in a most befitting way. In the form of destroying the enemies, protecting the subjects and establishing Hindu Dharma, King Kampana fulfils the first goal of life, i.e. *dharma*. Wherever Kampana becomes victorious in Kāñci, Madhurā, etc. he establishes stable and legal government for the welfare of the society.

---

[11] All the cantos are written in different metres using different *alaṁkāra*s – canto I: Anustubh metre; Canto II: Upajāti – sometimes Upendravajrā and Indrāvajrā metres'are also used; Canto III: Vaṁśastha metre; Canto IV: Anuṣṭubhmetre; Canto V: Drutavilambita metre; Canto VI: Puṣpitāgrā metre; Canto VII: Viyoginī metre; Canto VIII: Aupachandasika metre; Canto IX: Upajāti – sometimes Upendravajrā and Iridravajra and the subject matter of the following canto is suggested in the previous canto.

Carita-Kāvya

Madhurāvijayam is not only a *mahākāvya* but also a *carita-kāvya* and forms a part of biographical literature. Biography is a significant part of Sanskrit literature. It is a narrative, which records consciously and artistically, the important events happened in the life of a great person whom the author describes. The biographical works are the combination of history and literary art. So the biographer shares the historian a concern for truth and simultaneously shares originality with an ambition to create a work of art.

Biographical works are a significant treasure of Sanskrit literature. The life sketches or the biographies of important persons attracted many poets to write upon. Therefore, a huge number of *carita-kāvya*s have been composed. We have to accord due consideration to them as they possess high quality of literature. Although literary tradition in Sanskrit has been averse to the eulogy of a man, an exception seems to have been made in the case of saints and teachers in pre-modern times. This should explain the paucity of biographical literature in Sanskrit, during early and medieval times, and why the available writings of this genre relate to religious leaders and the ruler of the land. The earliest works in India, which could be termed biographical, occur in Buddhist literature written in Pāli, and they narrate the life story of the Buddha, i.e. *Buddhacarita*. Meaning, tradition of *carita-kāvya*s begins from Aśvaghoṣa who for the first time composed the great epic *Buddhacarita* in order to depict the life and teachings of the Buddha. The successors of Aśvaghoṣa readily accepted his immortal work as a model and continued to write *carita-kāvya*s of different types. The purpose behind such compositions is twofold. Besides providing aesthetic enjoyment to connoisseurs, the *carita-kāvya*s serve as a record of the activities of those persons who have made something good for the benefit of society or for the country. The *carita-kāvya*s thus unfold not only the history of those persons but also the conditions of the time, in which they had lived and worked. Further, in those parts of India where the tradition of historical writings did not develop, unlike Kashmir where Kalhaṇa's *Rājataraṅgiṇī* and its subsequent supplements came into being, that type of biographical writing provided a lot of historical facts and information to fill up the gaps in Indian history.

Sanskrit biographies have resulted in the introduction of poetic fancies and exaggerations in their composition. Biographies in Sanskrit, especially the early ones, have been composed long after the lifetime of the persons concerned, have the effect of introducing into them much legendary matter and hearsay accounts.

The word *carita* has the following meanings: performed, practised, attained, known, offered, going, moving course, acting, doing, practice, behaviour, acts, deeds, life, biography, adventures, history, story, behaviour, habit, conduct, acts, deeds, performance, observance, history, life, biography, account, adventure, nature, desposition and duty, established or instituted observance. For example:

udara-caritanam tu vasudhaiva kuṭumbakam,
scirvam khalasya caritam masakaḥ karoti,
uttarāram-caritaṁ tat praṇītam prayujyate.

So, some of the *carita-kāvya*s are historical, some are biographical, some are centring on the life of persons, some are on their deeds and some are on their characters. It is interesting to note that there are *carita-kāvya*s of many types and many forms. The objectives behind the compositions are also different.

Hence here *Madhurāvijayam* is also a *carita-kāvya* which is also called as *Vīra Kamparāyacarita* which is historical as well. The adventurous life and military exploits of Kampana who established the Vijayanagara Empire in Madurai – Tamil country. Though the contents of this poem mentioned in the above pages are biographical, the treatment is poetic, with the use of high-flown language, narrative style and eulogies it has descriptive narrations.

Influence of Sanskrit and Telugu Poets on Gaṅgādevī

At the beginning of *Madhurāvijayam*, Gaṅgādevī pays homage to some great poets in Sanskrit and Telugu. These thirteen stanzas (*MV* 1.4-16) are important in several respects. In her praise of each poet, she mentions in a brief way the most characteristic quality of the poet. These stanzas are assessments of the merits of the poet concerned and also what can be called as literary criticism. Among uncountable names in Sanskrit literature she chose only a very few poets whose works had immense influence on her. She paid rich tributes to those great poets such as Vālmīki, Vyāsa, Kālidāsa, Bāṇa Bhaṭṭa, Bhāravi, Daṇḍin, Bhavabhūti; specially from Āndhra region, such as Kriyāśakti, Līlāśuka, Tikkana, Agastya, Gaṅgādhara and her own *guru* Viśvanātha.

KRIYAŚAKTI

> I bow to teacher Kriyāśakti who has the great knowledge and to Goddess Sarvamaṅgalā who spends time with Trilocana who shines besides her. – *MV* 1.4

Immediately after the invocation of Gaṇeśa, Śiva, Pārvatī and Sarasvatī, she pays rich tributes to Kriyāśakti the *kulaguru* of Vijayanagara kingdom. She praises him as another Trilocana, unparlleled in wisdom and brilliance.

The fact that Kriyāśakti is mentioned even before Vālmīki shows his importance in the Vijayanagara royal family.

PRACETASA OR VĀLMĪKI

> May Sage Pracetasa who first set the erudition of creating poetry on earth, let him bring cheerfulness to the minds of the virtuous.
> – *MV* 1.5

> In every section of Vyāsa's sequence of expressions (the *Mahābhārata*), like the delicious juice in every joint of red sugar cane, there is sweet essence which convey immediate enjoyment to men of good taste. – *MV* 1.6

Vālmīki is mentioned as the first poet on the earth and as a *muni*. The implication is that, according to Gaṅgādevī, *prasāda* (lucidity) is the main characterstic of Vālmīki and Vyāsa. While praising Vyāsa, Gaṅgādevī compares his work, the *Mahābhārata*, to a sugar cane, because there is an aesthetic pleasure (*sāra*) in each *parva* of the *Mahābhārata*, just as there is sweet juice (*sāra*) in each segment (*parva*) of the sugar cane:

> *vaiyasake girām gumphe puṇḍrikṣav iva latihyate* ।
> *sadyaḥ sahṛdayīahlādi sāraḥ oarvāṇi parvani* ॥

Significantly, the last line of this stanza became a proverb in Āndhra. On the cover page of the Telugu *Mahābhārata*, they write even today *parvapi sāraḥ parvāni*, to which a new line is added, *pratiparva-rasāsvādam*.

KĀLIDĀSA

> Who are the poets who do not play the role of a slave to Kāldāsa? For, even the current peets live by his ideas. – *MV* 1.7

Gaṅgādevī was very much influenced by the works of Kālidāsa. Quite often she skilfully imitates Kālidāsa. Paying rich tributes to Kālidāsa:

> *dāsataṁ kālidāsasya kavayaḥ ke na bibhrati* ।
> *idānīṁ api tasyarthan upajivanty am yataḥ* ॥

To her, it is a merit of poetry to imitate Kālidāsa's poetry. Her deep study of Kālidāsa's works is seen in her use of tender expressions in the descriptions, in her poetic style. Especially, in Gaṅgādevī's descriptions of Vijayanagara, of the queen's pregnancy, Kampana's birth and childhood, we can see the clear influence of the *Raghuvaṁśa*. In the descriptions of the seasons she mostly follows the *Ṛtusaṁhāra* and *Meghadūta*. The descriptions of the dusk and the moon rise have similarities with such descriptions in the *Kumārasambhava*. The appearance of Goddess of Madurai and her naration of the miseries resembles the presiding deity of Ayodhyā telling her miseries to King Kuśa in *Raghuvaṁśa* 14.2.

Thus Gaṅgādevī echoed Kālidāsa's ideas throughout her poem, for her to imitate Kālidāsa is the sign of good poetry.

BAṆA BHAṬṬA

After Kālīdāsa, Gaṅgādevī pays tribute to Bāṇa Bhaṭṭa and praises in the following words:

> How could others grasp the expressiveness of Bāṇa Bhaṭṭa which captivates like the musical sound of the lute played by Sarasvatī's own hand. – *MV* 1.8

Her thorough study of the *Kādambarī* and the influence of Bāṇa Bhaṭṭa's works are reflected in *Madhurāvijayam*.

BHĀRAVI

> Just as the garland of *vakulā* flowers yields its sweet scent only when pressed, so too, the language of Bhāravi reveals its brilliance and gives delight to the erudite only if they perceive it. – *MV* 1.9

Gaṅgādevī says that just as a garland of *vakulā* flowers emits more fragrance after it is crushed again and again, even so Bhāravi's poem gives greater pleasure and more when one contemplates over it. Implied is the fact that there is a depth of meaning – *bhāravae arthaguravam* in Bhāravi's poetry. Bhāravi's influence can be seen in one or two places in *Madhurāvijayam*. In sixth canto, the water sports are described thus:

> In the pleasure lake the king splashed water on a lotus and this made a lady besides him cast on him angry looks of jealousy, along with the tears in the fringes of her eyes, so eyelashes were wet. The king, underneath the water, touched the upper part of a lady's thigh, she pretended it as if a fish-bite and hugged her lover even when her companions were looking on. – *MV* 6.57-58

DAṆḌIN

> Thriving of expressions of Ācārya Daṇḍin drunk (as it were) with the wealth of nectar, sparkle like the elegant precious gem-studded mirror of the creators consort. – *MV* 1.10

It is evidently said here that she has read the *Kāvyādarśa* of Daṇḍin and influenced by it, hence she describes Daṇḍin's expressions have the precious gems studded in the mirror.

BHAVABHŪTI

> I believe that Bhavabhūti's masterpieces must be some variety of Kāmadhenu, for they produce in the ears of the scholars a pleasure akin to the consumption of nectar. – *MV* 1.11

In her compliment to Bhavabhūti, Gaṅgādevī compares his composition to Kāmadhenu, for they produce in the ears of the scholars a pleasure just like the drinking of ambrosia.

LĪLĀŚUKA

Līlāśuka is believed to belong to Rolluru in Andhra Pradesh. He wrote the famous *Karṇāmṛta*. Gaṅgādevī compares his writings to the ocean of honey flowing from the flower clusters of the *mandāra* tree.

> Whom would the expressions of the poet of *Karṇāmṛta* fail to enchant by the expression of words like the ocean of honey flowing from the flower clusters of the *mandāra* tree? – *MV* 1.12

Whether Līlāśuka belonged to Āndhra or not, the following poets were definitely from the Āndhra region and they immensely influenced Gaṅgādevī, some of them were her contemporaries.

TIKKANA

Tikkana translated the last fifteen *parva*s of the *Mahābhārata* in Telugu. About him Gaṅgādevī says:

kaveḥ suktiḥ kaumudiva kalānidheḥ ।
satrsnaiḥ kavibhi svairm cakorair iva sevyate ।।

Even as the thirsty *cakora* birds love to drink the rays of the moon, poets find immense relishment in the poetic sayings of Tikkayya.
– *MV* 1.13

Tikkana belongs to the thirteenth century of the common era. He did a great service to Telugu literature by translating the Sanskrit *Mahābhārata* into Telugu. This translation of the great Sanskrit *Mahābhārata* into Telugu had an important role in Telugu literature. First, the *Mahābhārata* translation into Telugu language was started by Nannaya in the eleventh century but he translated only Ādi-Parva and some parts of Araṇya-Parva's only. In Telugu literature he is known as Ādikavi.

kiṁ asthimalara kiṁ kaustubhaṁ va pariṣkr̥yāyām jimanyase tvam ।
kiṁ klaklitaḥ kiṁ u va yaśodastanyam tava svadu vada prabho me ।।

This verse is significant for two reasons. First Tikkana shows his knowledge of Sanskrit. Second, by praising Hari (Viṣṇu) and Hara (Śiva) together, in the form of Harihara, he is criticizing the sectarian conflict between the followers of Śiva and worshippers of Viṣṇu.[12] Tikkana is propagating a synthesis of both religious sects. His teachings had influenced Vijayanagara kings, many of whom had the name Harihara. Gaṅgādevī very deeply studied Tikkana's works and those

[12] In the Telugu translation of the Virāṭa-Parva, there is a Sanskrit verse in praise of Harihara:

kim asthimalara kim kaustubham va pariskriyayam "Jimansye tvam ।
kim klaklitah kim u va yasodastanyam tava svadu vada prabho me ।।
Āndhramahābhārata, Virāṭa-Parva 1.10

works highly inspired her. In *Madhurāvijayam* the influence of Tikkana can be seen in the ninth canto.

But, between the eleventh and fourteenth centuries, the *Mahābhārata* was translated into Telugu by Nannaya, Tikkana and Errana. Nannaya translated the Ādi and Sabhā-Parva and a part of the Araṇya-Parva, which was completed by Errana in the fourteenth century. Tikkana translated the remaining fifteen *parva*s, starting from the Virāṭa. As Nannaya and Tikkana compared the armed forces to rivers and oceans, Gaṅgādevī also compares forces to rivers and oceans. During his advice to Kampana, Bukka says:

> *sahasrasas tuṅgaturaṅgavicayo madavipadvlpa viśeśitintarah* ।
> *bhāvantam ugrayudhanakrarājayo bhajanti nityam bahuḷa balabdayah* ।।

Here the poet compares the army to the ocean, horses in thousands act as its waves, elephants are like huge islands and the destructive weapons are like crocodiles in the waters. The same idea about armies had been described before her by Nannaya in the *Mahābhārata*.

At another place, Gaṅgādevī describes the army as the ocean in which the horses with their foaming mouths and wind-like steeds looked just like the waves. The same idea was given by Tikkana in his *Mahābhārata* in Bhīṣma-Parva.

The *Mahābhārata* is mainly famous for its fearsome and gruesome battle between the Kauravas and the Pāṇḍavas. In the Telugu *Mahābhārata* Tikkana with his own experience directly or indirectly with battlefields described the battle very vividly and beautifully. Its influence on Gaṅgādevī can be seen in the ninth canto very clearly.

She describes the armies or the battlefield or the battle itself; the inspiration of Tikkana can be seen in her poem. Battle between the horse to horse, elephant to elephant and about the blood rivers in the battlefield, pearls from the broken heads of elephants attacked by heroic warriors, etc. were described lucidly in the ninth canto.

According to poetics, in a *mahākāvya*, there must be vivid description of the dawn and dusk. It is a common feature of Telugu poets, that they are always very nearer to the nature in describing the beautiful landscapes of the dawn and the dusk. This influence can be seen in Gaṅgādevī also. About the dusk she illustrates:

Then the sun as if frightened of the fault he had given to the queens by making lotuses emulate the beauty of their faces sunk into the caverns of western mountains. From there he submerged into the waters of western ocean as if to replenish his heat from the underwater heat, the heat which had been spent in the day in making lotuses blossom.

– *MV* 7.1-2

AGASTYA[13]

Who will not be jealous of the breathless (writings) of the man of learning of the poet Agastya whose wealth of learning is established by the creation of as many as seventy-four poetic compositions?

– *MV* 1.14

Agastya also belonged to Āndhradeśa. He was a court poet of Kākatīya King Pratāparudra Deva II of Warangal (1294–1325 CE) and was probably patronized by Saṅgama and Bukka I of Viajayanagara. As a master of literary art, Gaṅgādevī mentions him as the author of seventy-four *kāvya*s and as a poet of great versatality. He became famous by name of Vidyānātha, because of his scholarship. And under that name he wrote the famous book *Pratāparudrayaśobhūṣaṇa* on poetics. Gaṅgādevī praises him as follows:

catuhsaptatikavyoktivyāktavaidusyasaṁpade ǀ
agastyaya jagaty astnin spr̥hyet ko na kavidah ǁ

Agastya, apart from the *Pratāparudrayaśobhūṣaṇa,* has written the *Bālabhārata* (poem in twenty cantos), *Kr̥ṣṇacarita* (prose on the life of Lord Kr̥ṣṇa), *Nalakīrtikaumudī* (poem on Nala, only two cantos are available).

GAṄGĀDHARA

We reverentially treat the great poet Gaṅgādhara as the second Vyāsa. In that he has made the story of the Bharata as the visual poetry – which enacted as drama.

– *MV* 1.15

Gaṅgādhara was the husband of Agastya's sister. Gaṅgādevī adored him as the second Vyāsa, because he dramatized the *Mahābhārata* story. Most probably he was the author of the two play: the *Candravilāsa* and *Rāghavābyudaya.*

---

[13] The name Agastya is a tradition in south India and even considered as one among the Prajāpatis.

VIŚVANĀTHA

> May the lord of the poet Viśvanātha prosper for long, it is by his grace, even in individuals like myself, has dawned an everlasting sense of poetry. – *MV* 1.16

Viśvanātha was the *guru* of Gaṅgādevī. Describing him as *kavīśvara* she prays for his longevity, it shows that he was of ripe old age when she learnt from him; she says that it is only through his grace even individuals like her have become scholars in all Śāstras and Kāvyas of Sanskrit literature.

ciram sa vijayi bhuylit visvanath. kaviśvaraḥ ।
yasya prāsadat sarvajjnyaṁ samindhe madrsesva api ॥

Viśvanātha also belonged to Orugalu, modern Warangal. He was also a court poet of Pratāparudradeva to entertain an assembly of scholars at Kākatīya court. He wrote a one-act play *Saugaṅdhikaharaṇa.*

rājna prataparudradeva sambhavitair aśeṣa-vidye
viśeṣa-sarasarvañjnadhaureya-matihbiḥ sabhasadbhir
iihuya sabahumanam ādiṣṭo smi
viśvanatha iti khyāta kavir astu yaduktayaḥ
akañcanam aratnam ca vidūṣam karṇabhuṣana

Under his able direction, Gaṅgādevī became a versatile genius. Agastya and Viśvanātha influenced Gaṅgādevī very much and made her write this beautiful poem *Madhurāvijayam*. Agastya was Viśvanātha's maternal uncle and Gaṅgādhara was his father. Viśvanātha praises his maternal uncle Agastya in the following verse:

vacas tasya kaver udaramadhura ity atra citraṁ kiṁ u
prākhyatah sakalāsu dīkṣu guṇiṣu śreyan agastyah suahiḥ
vedscandramukhi-karaṅgulidalasaṅgakvanād-vallaki
vacoyukti-sahoktal-dārśita-sudhājarmtia sa yan mātulaḥ

So far as the present *mahākāvya* is concerned, we can distinguish narrations from descriptions on the basis of the attitude of the poetess. Those portions of this *mahākāvya* which narrate the various incidents of the story and also those which tend to carry the *kathā-vastu* of a *mahākāvya* further and serve as a connecting link between what precedes it and what follows it should be counted as narrations.

There is no doubt that narration holds a subordinate position in this *mahākāvya*, the major portion being occupied by descriptions. Gaṅgādevī's *Madhurāvijayam* is a *mahākāvya*, in which descriptions occupy a major portion as compared to narrations. The narrations are very brief and are presented in a summarized form.

Religion

Śaivism was the main religion of Saṅgama dynasty although some population worshipped Viṣṇu. It was Śiva who was propitiated by royalty. Lord Śiva is invoked in the opening verses of the *mahākāvya Madhurāvijayam*. As depicted by the poetess, their *kulaguru* Kriyāśakti was an ardent devotee of Lord Śiva. Besides the existence of the temple of the Virūpākṣa in the suburb of Pampā it hints that Lord Śiva was an adorable deity of the Vijayanagara kings:

> Meant for attaining knowledge in the creation who has adored in the forms of man and woman that God Śiva and his wife, who personify the universal consciousness I pray to them and entirely come near to them. – *MV* 1.2

> I bow to teacher Kriyāśakti who has the great knowledge and to Goddess Sarvamaṅgalā who spends time with Trilocana who shines besides her. – *MV* 1.4

> Pampā was the branch city of Vijaya. Many wealthy lords lived there so much so that God Virūpākṣa who was enshrined there never thought about his original home at the city of Alakā. – *MV* 1.66

The images of Hariharanātha represent a combination of Hari and Hara marking the final synthesis of the two opposing cults of Vaiṣṇavism and Śaivism. The Harihara cult was symbolic of the spirit of toleration that prevailed during this period. There was a temple dedicated to God Harihara at Hampī. The Vīraśaiva divinities (or gods) and their philosophy inspired much of the Kannada literature of this period. The theme of the Kannada works centred round Śiva and his *līlā*s, the Śaivite saints, the Nāyanars of the south, miracles performed by Basavanna and his followers, the supreme sanctity of the *Pañcākṣarī*, etc. illustrate that Śaivism was stronger than any other religion. The name of the king Harihara is itself an example of practising of this tradition. However, it must be accepted that the empire did create conditions of security for Hindu culture and institutions and it succeeded in limiting the expansion of Muslim power in the Deccan for over two centuries. During this period the outlook of the Hindus of the south developed an orthodoxy in social and religious matters. The encouragement of religion by the Vijayanagara monarchs, as revealed by numerous inscriptions, included the promotion of Vedic and other in cultures, support of brāhmaṇas, generous patronage was extended to *maṭha*s and temples, pilgrimages to religious places and celebration of religious festivals and public rituals were in vogue.

Ecology: Habit and Habitat

The eco system of the period is well represented through the description of landscapes. The text mentions almost all types of flora and fauna occurred in that geographic limits of Madurai, Kāñcī and its surroundings.

The text primarily mentions the riverine delta of Kāverī, Tuṅgabhadrā and Tāmraparṇī along with other rivers such as Palar. These riverine deltas have been portrayed as rich in crop production. The crops mainly grown were paddy and other cereals. In between the water terrains, the mountainous terrain is also well represented.

Gaṅgādevī while describing Hampī, the capital of Vijayanagara Empire, refers that it is surrounded by banana orcharos, beautiful mansions and artificial garden mountains that are called as play mountains:

> The pleasure mountains in the city were frequented by the musk deer that sought the shade of the banana plants and *karpūra* plants in these hillocks looked like the genuine hiding place of the god of love. – *MV* 1.48

> Though she was physically unable to walk as far as the pleasure hill where the deer were quietly grazing, she in her mental flights was on the pinnacle of the Malaya Mountain populated by ferocious lions. – *MV* 2.6

These play mountains were used to be situated near the royal harems to enable the inhabitants of the palace to play different games and for evening walks.

Gaṅgādevī mentions that the Mount Cakrācala surrounded the capital Vidyānagara:

> The city was also surrounded by ramparts on all sides which were as high as the Cakrācala mountains and it had the beauty of the water channels surrounded by the Lakṣmī creeper and looked like the navel of Goddess Earth. – *MV* 1.45

It also represents a mythical mountain and believed to be the residence of various gods. The Mandāra Mountain was served as a churning stick at the time of churning the ocean for the purpose of obtaining nectar by both gods and demons. So Mandāra is an imaginary mountain. Gaṅgādevī compares the march of the army of Prince Kampana with that of the sound emerged at the time of churning the ocean with Mandāra Mountain. The Malaya Mountain is mentioned to mean the mountain range on the part of the country:

> As he marched in state, King Kampana caused a tremble in the hearts of his rivals and turned to the direction of the quarter which had the Malaya Mountain for its boundary. – *MV* 4.34

Gaṅgādevī presents a beautiful picture of the summer season. Naturally the sun moves towards northern direction during summer. She conceives the movement of the sun to north as a lover, unable to bear the heat of separation from his beloved, moves towards the abode of snow (Himācala) located in the northern direction.

Sumeru is one of the highest peaks of the Himalayas which is said to be the residence of the *vidyādhara*s. Gaṅgādevī compares the height of the mansions of Vijayanagara with that of the peaks of Meru Mountain.

> Lofty and gem-set towers, like the peaks of the mount Sumeru emanating rainbow colours, ornamented the city. – *MV* 1.46

Kālindaja is the name of River Yamunā, derived from the very characteristics of its waters. As the water in the river seems to be black in colour the river that flows in the northern part of the country is named as Kālindaja. Gaṅgādevī describes:

> There was smoke rising from the cooling down of the sun's rays on earth surface; there beetles disguised as night darkness filling that region after leaving the closed lotuses; the black waters of the rivers were rising as tall as trees resembling the disturbances of the Yamunā River created by Śrī Kṛṣṇa at the time of Kālīya-mardana. – *MV* 7.25

This also draws our attention to the mythological origination of River Yamunā. According to it, Balarāma brought out the River Yamunā with his weapon plough to form a separate river for the utility of his people. And it is also called Kālinda, because it was said to have got its origin from the mountain of Kālinda.

Gaṅgādevī refers the Milky ocean with:

> The quarters then shone with spotless gleam as if they had been newly washed by royal fame which was fit to be likened to the whiteness of milk that filled the milky ocean. – *MV* 2.15

> Then in course of time the queen bore to the king two other sons called Kampana and Saṅgama who were like *pārijāta* and *cintāmaṇi* that sprang from the milky ocean. – *MV* 2.40

She concieves the ocean of milk as it is common to poets to attribute whiteness to the objects of purity hence the froth of the ocean is compared to the sea of milk, where Lord Viṣṇu is said to have always reclined on the bed of Ādi-Śeṣa. Because of its saltiness Gaṅgādevī addresses it as:

> Horses neighing along with the white froth, seemed to ridicule at Hanumān who took great pleasure in having merely crossed the saltish ocean. – *MV* 4.24

Gaṅgādevī makes a reference to Arabian Sea while describing the setting of the sun in the seventh canto:

> The reddish of twilight-like tender leaves began to appear in the western horizon in the form of coral reefs given out by the western ocean in the disturbance caused by the rapid descend once of the sun into its depth. – *MV* 7.22

Gaṅgādevī refers to River Tuṅgabhadrā that flew through the kingdom of Vijayanagara Empire:

> As if in rivalry with the heavenly waters that flowed round the borders of heaven, River Tuṅgabhadrā surrounded the city as a terrible moat. – *MV* 1.44

In fact, they are two separate rivers Tuṅga and Bhadrā. Both originate from the western part of the Karnataka state. They merge into one and called as Tuṅgabhadrā and then merge into Kṛṣṇā River.

There is a description of Tāmraparṇī which flows near Madhurā and is compared to Tuṅgabhadrā:

> Without considering River Tuṅgabhadrā which flowed nearby and which was easily fordable she desired to sport in the Tāmraparṇī in the company of her army of elephants that would raise waves in its waters (while they played in the water). – *MV* 2.5

> The waters of Tāmraparṇī which were once white with sandal paste rubbed away from the breasts of charming young women are now flowing red with the blood of cows slaughtered by the miscreants. – *MV* 8.11

At present, Tāmraparṇī rises from the Western Ghāṭs, through the district of Tirunelvelly, and falls into the gulf of Mannar.

> The River Kāverī, uncurbed by proper *bāndha*s (dams), has become deflected very much from her time-honoured course, and flows in all sorts of wrong directions as if imitating the Turuṣkas in their actions. – *MV* 8.5

It is said that the Sage Agastya brought Gaṅgā in his *kamaṇḍalu* and dropped it on the Sahyādri mountain. From that day it flows from that mountain and it was known as Sahyakanyā. Presently, it is popularly called Kāverī in southern part of the country flowing from western part of Karnataka state to the eastern end of Tamil Nadu, and is also known as Dakṣiṇagaṅgā.

Gaṅgādevī makes a reference to Kṣirataraṅgiṇī, a river in south India.

> The dust raised by his army made both the Palar and the fame of the Śambuvarāya monarch look grimy. – *MV* 4.49

The river locally known as "Paleru" meaning a river of milk. On the northern bank of this river, there is Kāñcīpuram, one of the seven ancient cities of India for its sanctity. Gaṅgādevī refers many a time the oceans that surround the southern peninsula. Mythologically the abode of Viṣṇu is conceived as the ocean of milk; the ocean is also called *lavaṇa samudra* as its water is always salty in taste and also known as *paścima-samudra* from this epithet Vijayanagara kings were addressed *paścimasamudradīśa*. While describing the sunsets in the west, in Arabian Sea, as it lies on the western part of the country *paścima-samudra* is used.

Data on various trees and plants are available in *Madhurāvijayam*. It is said that there were plants known as *kalpapādapa* which were abundant.

> Let it be prosperous to God, who has protruded teeth in the face (Gaṇeśa). Whose form is like the *kalpa* plants, fulfils the desires of the shelter seekers of those that surrender to his elegance, be auspicious to the good. – *MV* 1.1

The word *kalpa* meaning ritual and *pādapa* meaning tree or plant. The simple meaning of this is plants and its products used in rituals. It is natural that these plants have been attributed divinity because these are used in rituals and also other meaning of *kalpa* in folk or popular oral literature is that "All the parts of a plant which are useful for human beings." Example is a coconut tree which is termed as *kalpavṛkṣa*. All parts of which are useful in one or the other way and is abundantly used for ritual purposes. The other plants which are mentioned are lotus, *campaka*, jasmine, hibiscus and other flowering plants.

This above analysis of the text gives a mine of information and the authorship of this text by a poetess, given at the end of every canto, which confirms the authorship of Queen Gaṅgādevī.[14]

---

[14] *Gaṅgadevī Viracitam.*

Bibliography

Primary Sanskrit Texts

Acyutarāyābhyudayam of Śrī Rājanātha Diṇḍima, ed. R.V. Krishnamachariar, Srirangam, 1907.

Gaṅgādevī's Madhurāvijayam, ed. Tiruvenkatachari, Annamalainagar: Annamalai University, 1957.

Kāvyamīmāṁsā of Rājaśekhara, Original Text in Sanskrit and Translation with Explanatory Notes by Sadhana Parashar, New Delhi: D.K. Printworld, 2000.

Madhurāvijayam or Vīra Kamparāyacarita: A Historical Kāvya by Gaṅgādevī, ed. G. Harihara Śāstrī and V. Śrīnivāsa Śāstrī, 2nd edn, Trivandrum: Sanskrit Publication Department, 1924.

Paddhati of *Śārṅgadhara* VI: *The Text*, 1888, ed. Peter Peterson, reprint edn, Cambridge: Kessinger Publishing, 2010.

Ramabhadramba, *Raghunāthābhyudaya,* ed. T.R. Chintamani: University of Madras, 1934.

Subhāṣitaratnakośa, tr. D.H.H. Ingalls, Harvard University Press, Harvard Oriental Series, 1965.

Subhāṣitāvalī of Vallabhadeva, ed. Peter Peterson, Pandit Durgaprasad, Bombay Sanskrit Series 31, Bombay, 1886.

Tirumalāmbā, *Ambikāpariṇaya Campū,* tr. into Hindi by Pandit Giridhara Sharma Caturvedi, ed. Laxman Sarup, Motilal Banarsidass, Punjab Samskrita Pustakalaya Lahore, 1920/22.

Tirumalāmbā's "Ambikāpariṇaya", in *Proceedings of the Fifth Indian Oriental Conference*, vol. I, Lahore: University of Punjab, 1930.

Tirumalāmbā, *Varadāmbikāpariṇaya Campū,* tr. and ed. Surya Kantha Sastri, Varanasi: Choukamba Samskrita Series Office, 1970.

Vijaya Vilāsamu of Cemakuri Venkatakavi (Telugu).

Secondary Sources

Aiyangar, Krishnaswamy, 1919, *Sources of Vijayanagara History,* New Delhi: Aryan Publishers, 2003 reprint.

Aiyangar, Krishnasvami S., et al., 2000, *Vijayanagara History and Legacy*, Delhi: Aryan Book International.

Aiyangar, M.T. Narasimha, 1908, "Madhuravāṇī: The Sanskrit Poetess of Tanjore", in *The Indian Review*, February, pp. 106-11.

Anila Varghese, 1995, *Religious Traditions at Vijayanagara* (*as Revealed through Its Monuments*), New Delhi: American Institute of Indian Studies.

Basu, K.K., 1936, "The Battle of Taḷīkōta: Before and After", in *Vijayanagara Sexcentenary Commemoration Volume*, pp. 245-54, Dharwar: Vijayanagara Sexcentenary Association.

Cosman, Carol et al., 1979, *The Penguin Book of Women Poets*, London: Viking Press.

Chaudhuri, J.B. (ed.), 2001, *The Contribution of Women to Sanskrit Literature,* 3 vols, New Delhi: Cosmo Publications.

Dallapiccola, Anna L., 1992, *The Ramachandra Temple at Vijayanagara,* Vijayanagara Research Project Monograph Series, New Delhi: Manohar.

Dallapiccola, Anna L. and Anila Verghese, 1998, *Sculpture at Vijayanagara: Iconography and Style,* Vijayanagara Research Project Monograph Series 6, New Delhi: Manohar.

Dallapiccola, Anna L. and Stephanie Zingel-Avé Lallemant, 1985, *Vijayanagara, City and Empire: New Currents of Research,* 2 vols, Beiträge zür Südasienforschung 100, Stuttgart: Steiner.

Dallapiccola, Anna L. (ed.), 1992, *Vijayanagara: City and Empire*, 2 vols, Stuttgart: Franz Steine Verlag.

Davison-Jenkins, Dominic J., 1997, *The Irrigation and Water Supply Systems of Vijayanagara,* Vijayanagara, Research Project Monograph Series 5, New Delhi: Manohar.

Desai P.B., 1936, *Vijayanagara Sāmrājya* (Kannada), Dharwar: Vijayanagara Smarakotsva Samiti.

———, 1981, *A History of Karnataka*, rev. edn, Dharwad: Kannada Research Institute, Karnataka University.

Devaraja D.V. and C.S. Patil (eds), 1996, *Vijayanagara Progress of Research, Report 1987-88*, Mysore: Directorate of Archaeology and Museums.

———, *Report 1988-91*, Mysore: Directorate of Archaeology and Museums.

Devaraj, D.V. and S. Chennabasappa Patil (eds), 1996, *Vijayanagara Adhyayana*, vol. I, first edn, Mysore: Directorate of Archaeology and Museums.

Dimmit, Cornelia and J.A.B. Van Buitenen (eds and trs), 1978, *Classical Hindu Mythology: A Reader in the Sanskrit Puranas,* Philadelphia: Temple University Press.

Dirks, Nicholas B., 1976, "Political Authority and Structural Change in Early South Indian History", *The Indian Economic and Social History Review*, vol. 13(2): 125-57.

Dikshit, G.S, 1988, *Early Vijayanagara Studies in Its History and Culture*, Bangalore: B.M. Sri Smaraka Pratishtana.

Davison-Jenkins, Dominic J., 1997, *The Irrigation and Water Supply Systems of Vijayanagara,* first edn, New Delhi: American Institute of Indian Studies.

Duarte, Barbosa, 1918, *The Book of Duarte Barbosa*, tr. with notes Longworth Dames, 2 vols, London: The Hakluyt Society.

Filliozat, Pierre Sylvain and Vasundhara Filliozat, 1988, *Hampi-Vijayanagar: The Temple of Viṭṭhala,* New Delhi: Sitaram Bhartia Institute of Scientific Research.

Filliozat, Vasundhara, 1973, *L'épigraphie de Vijayanagar du début à 1377*, Publications de l'Ecole Française d'Extrême-Orient 91, Paris: École Française d'Extrême-Orient.

———, 1976, *Hampi* (Kannada), Lecture Series 238, Dharwar: Karnataka University.

———, 1977, *The Vijayanagara Empire as Seen by Domingo Paes and Fernao Nuniz*, New Delhi: National Book Trust.

———, 1980, *Vijayanagara Sāmrājya Sthapane* (Kannada), Bangalore: Kannada Sahitya Parishat.

Filliozat, Vasundhara and George Michell, 1981, *Splendours of the Vijayanagara Empire, Hampi*, Bombay: Marg Publications.

Fritz, John M., George Michell and M.S. Nagaraja Rao, 1984, *Where Kings and Gods Meet: The Royal Centre at Vijayanagara, India,* Tucson, AZ: University of Arizona Press.

Gollings, John, John M. Fritz and George Michell, 1991, *City of Victory, Vijayanagara: The Medieval Hindu Capital of Southern India,* New York: Aperture.

Gopal, B.R., 1985, *Vijayanagara Inscriptions,* Centenary Publication no. 3, Mysore: Directorate of Archaeology and Museums.

Hall, Kenneth R., 2001, *Structure and Society in Early South India, Essays in Honour of Noburu Karashima,* Delhi: Oxford University Press.

Hayavadana Rao, C., 1930, "Vijayanagara Kingdom", *Mysore Gazetteer*, vol. II, part 3, Bangalore: Government Press.

Heras, Henry, 1927, *The Aravidu Dynasty of Vijayanagara,* Madras: B.G. Paul and Co.

———, 1929, *Beginings of Vijayanagara History*, 1st edn, Bombay: Indian Historical Research Institute.

Hymavathi, P., 1994, *Vijayanagara: The Life and Times of Tuluva Vīra Narasiṁharāya,* Madras: New Era Publications.

Kalburgi, M.M. (ed.), 1994, *Karnatakada Kaifiyattugalu* (Kannada), Hampi: Kannada University.

Kaul, Shonaleeka, 2006, "Women about Town: An Exploration of Sanskrit Kavya Tradition", *Studies in History*, n.s., 22(1): 59-76.

Konduri, Sarojini Devi, 1990, *Religion in Vijayanagara Empire*, New Delhi: Sterling Publishers.

Kotraiah, C.T.M., 1995, *Irrigation Systems under Vijayanagara Empire*, Mysore: Directorate of Archaeology and Museums.

———, 1998, *Hampeyalli Virashaiva Prachina Kuruhugalu* (Kannada), unpublished, Agadi Sanganna Memorial, Koppal.

Kotrayya, S.M., 1961, *A Glorious Past*, Souvenir, 25th Year Anniversary of the Syndicate Bank, Hospet Branch, pp. 1-6, Hospet: Syndicate Bank.

Krishnaswami, A., 1964, *The Tamil Country under Vijayanagara*, Annamalainagar: The Annamalai University.

Longhurst, A.H., 1925, *Hampi Ruins: Described and Illustrated,* 2nd edn, Calcutta: Government of India.

Mahalingam, T.V., 1940, *Administration and Social Life under Vijayanagara,* Madras University Historical Series 15, Madras: University of Madras.

Mahalingam, T.V., 1942 (1969), *Administration and Social Life under Vijayanagara*, parts I and II, Madras: University of Madras.

———, 1977, *Readings in South Indian History*, Delhi: B.R. Publishing Corporation.

Meister, Michael W. and Madhusudan A. Dhaky, 1983, *Encyclopedia of Indian Temple Architecture,* Philadelphia: American Institute of Indian Studies.

Mitchell, George, 1988, *The Hindu Temple: An Introduction to Its Meaning and Forms,* Chicago: University of Chicago Press.

———, 1992, *The Vijayanagara Courtly Style: Incorporation and Synthesis in the Royal Architecture of Southern India, 15th–17th Centuries*, Vijayanagara Research Project Monograph Series, New Delhi: American Institute of Indian Studies.

———, 1995, *Architecture and Art of Southern India: Vijayanagara and the Successor States*, New Cambridge History of India 1; The Mughals and Their Contemporaries, Cambridge: Cambridge University Press.

———, 2000, *Hindu Art and Architecture, World of Art*, London: Thames and Hudson.

Mitchell, George and M.S. Nagaraja Rao, 1990, *Vijayanagara, Architectural Inventory of the Urban Core,* Vijayanagara Research Centre Series 5, Mysore: Directorate of Archaeology and Museums.

Morrison, Kathleen D., 2000, *Fields of Victory: Vijayanagara and the Course of Intensification,* Delhi: Munshiram Manoharlal.

Nagaraja Rao, M.S. and George Michell, 1983, *Vijayanagara, Progress of Research, 1979-1983*, Vijayanagara Research Centre Series 1, Mysore: Directorate of Archaeology and Museums.

———, 1985, *Vijayanagara, Progress of Research, 1983-1984*, Centenary Publication 1, Mysore: Directorate of Archaeology and Museums.

Narasimhamurthy, A.V., 1991, *Coins and Currency System in Vijayanagara Empire,* Numismatic Notes and Monographs 21, Varanasi: Numismatic Society of India.

Nelatur Venkataramanayya, 1972, *Krishna Devarāyalu* (Telugu), Hyderabad: Andhra Pradesh Prabutvalu.

Nilakanta Sastri, K.A. and N. Venkata Ramanayya, 1946, *Further Sources of Vijayanagara History,* Madras University Historical Series 18, Madras: University of Madras.

Nuniz, Fernao, 1991, *Chronicle of Fernao Nuniz*, tr. R. Sewell, Forgotten Empire, pp. 291-395, New Delhi/Madras: Asian Educational Services.

Patil, Channabasappa S. and Vinoda C. Patil, 1995, *Inscriptions at Vijayanagara* (*Hampi*), Inscriptions of Karnataka 1, Mysore: Directorate of Archaeology and Museums.

Paes, Domingo, 1991, *Narrative of Domingo Paes*, tr. Robert Sewell, Forgotten Empire, pp. 236-93, New Delhi/Madras: Asian Educational Services.

Pollock, Sheldon (ed.), 2003, *Literary Cultures in History: Reconstructions from South Asia,* Berkeley: University of California Press.

———, 1998, "India in the Vernacular Millennium: Literary Culture and Polity, 1000–1500", *Daedalus*, 127(3): 41-74.

Rao, V.N. et al., 1992, *Symbols of Substance: Court and State in Nayaka Period Tamilnadu*, Delhi: Oxford University Press.

———, 2001, *Textures of Time: Writing History in South India, 1600–1800*, Delhi: Permanent Black.

Saletore, Bhasker Anand, 1934, *Social and Political Life in the Vijayanagara Empire (AD 1346–AD 1646)*, Madras: B.G. Paul and Co.

———, 1938, *Mediaeval Jainism: With Special Reference to the Vijayanagara Empire,* Bombay: Karnataka Publishing House.

Saletore, Rajaram Narayan, 1982, *Vijayanagara Art,* Delhi: Sundeep Prakashan.

Saraswathi Nanaiah, N., 1992, *The Position of Women During Vijayanagara Period, 1336–1646*, Mysore: Southern Printers.

Sarma, Sreerama, P., 1979, *Saluva Dynasty of Vijayanagara,* Hyderabad: Prabhakar Publications.

Sarup, Lakshman, 1953, "A Queen Poetess of Vijayanagara", in *Festschrift moritz Winternitz,* ed. Otto Stein and Wilhelm Gampert, Leipzig: Otto Harrassowitz.

Sathanathiar, R., 1956, *Studies in the Ancient History of Toṇḍaimaṅḍalaṁ*, Madras: University of Madras.

Sewell, Robert, 1970, *A Forgotten Empire: Vijayanagar: A Contribution to the History of India,* New Delhi: National Book Trust.

Shah, Shalini, 2008, "Poetesses in Classical Sanskrit Literature", *Indian Journal of Gender Studies*, 15(1): 1-27.

———, 2009, *Love, Eroticism and Female Sexuality in Classical Sanskrit Literature, Seventh–Thirteenth Centuries*, New Delhi: Manohar.

Sinopoli, Carla M., 1993, *Pots and Palaces: The Earthenware Ceramics of the Noblemen's Quarter of Vijayanagara,* Vijayanagara Research Project Monograph Series 1, New Delhi: Manohar.

Sivaramamurti, C., 1985, *Vijayanagara Paintings,* New Delhi: Publications Division, Ministry of Information and Broadcasting.

Stein, B., 1980, *Peasant State and Society in Medieval South India,* New Delhi: Oxford University Press.

———, 1989, *Vijayanagara: New Cambridge History of India*, Cambridge: Cambridge University Press.

Tharu, Susie and K. Lalitha (eds), 1993, *Women Writing in India from 600 BC to the Early Twentieth Century*, 2 vols, New York: Feminist Press.

Venkata Ramanayya, N., 1929, *Kampili and Vijayanagara*, Madras: Christian Literature Society's Press.

———, 1933, *Vijayanagara: Origin of the City and the Empire*, Madras: University of Madras.

———, 1935, *Studies in the Third Dynasty of Vijayanagara,* Madras: University of Madras.

———, 1946, *Further Sources of Vijayanagara History*, Madras: University of Madras.

Venkatarathnam, A.V., 1972, *Local Self Government in the Vijayanagara Empire*, first edn, Mysore: University of Mysore.

Verghese, Anila, 1995, *Religious Traditions at Vijayanagara, as Revealed Through Its Monuments,* Vijayanagara Research Project Monograph Series 4, New Delhi: Manohar and American Institute of Indian Studies.

———, 2000, *Archaeology, Art and Religion: New Perspectives on Vijayanagara*, Delhi: Oxford University Press.

Vriddhagirisan, V., 1942, *The Nayakas of Tanjore*, Annamalainagar: Annamala University, reprint 1995, New Delhi: Asian Educational Services.